AFTER FORTY YEARS
HOW TO AVOID THE PITFALLS OF BOATING

DAVE WHEELER

BRISTOL FASHION PUBLICATIONS, INC.
Rockledge, Florida

After Forty Years --- Dave Wheeler

Published by Bristol Fashion Publications, Inc.

Copyright © 2002 by David Wheeler. All rights reserved.

No part of this book may be reproduced or used in any form or by any means-graphic, electronic, mechanical, including photocopying, recording, taping or information storage and retrieval systems-without written permission of the publisher.

BRISTOL FASHION PUBLICATIONS AND THE AUTHOR HAVE MADE EVERY EFFORT TO INSURE THE ACCURACY OF THE INFORMATION PROVIDED IN THIS BOOK BUT ASSUMES NO LIABILITY WHATSOEVER FOR SAID INFORMATION OR THE CONSEQUENCES OF USING THE INFORMATION PROVIDED IN THIS BOOK.

ISBN: 1-892216-44-2
LCCN: 2002116256

Contribution acknowledgments

Cover Design: John P. Kaufman
Cover Photo: Dave Wheeler
Interior Graphics & Photos: Dave Wheeler

After Forty Years --- Dave Wheeler

After Forty Years --- Dave Wheeler

DEDICATION

Books take a lot of work, not only by the author but by people who helped in many different ways. My list starts with Andree Conrad, the editor at *Southern Boating* who bought my first marine articles. David Strickland provided counsel and guidance for my articles when he took over as the next editor of *Southern Boating*.

The United States Power Squadrons and their excellent educational programs gave me a solid background to work with. My good friend, Harry Holmbraker, always arrived to save my computer from some of the ill-advised moves I made. Certainly not least is my wife, Jan, who fed, fetched, encouraged and edited while I pounded the keys.

After Forty Years --- Dave Wheeler

INTRODUCTION

This book starts with some of the foolish things we did as we tried to learn how to operate a boat without knowing what we were doing. Admittedly, some people survive and profit through disaster. We had friends who were overcome with the marine passion, bought a sailboat and started out on their first cruise headed for Tahiti. They survived but it was painful and expensive. You can do that too -- if you have more testosterone and money than brains. Looking back now, we can guarantee there are easier ways to start out.

No matter how old and grizzled they may be, all boaters are romantics at heart. They dream of white sails and blue skies but they never think of stormy weather or problems with rigging or machinery. They fail to realize that keeping a boat afloat eventually demands knowledge of many things they never intended to do. Sooner or later they get lessons in engine maintenance, plumbing, electricity, painting, varnishing and dozens of the prosaic and practical marine realities.

This is a book based on our learning experiences. I hope you find it helpful and it enables you to manage better than we did.

David Wheeler

After Forty Years --- Dave Wheeler

After Forty Years --- Dave Wheeler

TABLE OF CONTENTS

Introduction   7

Chapter One - *The Boats*   17
    Sailing lessons
    Switching to power
    Dinghies
    38 Egg Harbor
    41 Egg Harbor Motoryacht
    43 Viking Double Cabin
    50 Ocean Alexander

Chapter Two - *Maintenance*   33
    Cruising Religion
    Engine room
    Generator
    Changing Filters
    Seacocks
    Double Base for Pumps

Chapter Three – *Electrical*   43
    Wiring
    Connections
    Surge Protectors
    Electrical Distribution
    Monitoring
    12 Volt Power

Chapter Four – *Varnish & Paint*   53
    Varnishing Teak
    Furniture Strippers
    Chip Brushes
    Water Based Paints & Varnishes

Chapter Five - *Marine Interiors*   63
    Refinishing
    Marine Fabrics

Chapter Six - *Plumbing*   73
    The Head
    Paper Towels
    Water Heaters

Chapter Seven - *The Galley*   77
    Galley Tile
    Louvered Galley Cabinets
    Galley Tips
    Preserving Plates & Cups

Chapter Eight - *Air Conditioning*   81
    Keeping Cool
    Insulation
    Ventilation

Chapter Nine – *Telephones*   87
    Land Lines
    Seagoing cellular

Chapter Ten – *Pests*   93
    Bugs
    Blind mosquitoes

Chapter Eleven - *Little Things*   99
    Fiddles & Caps
    The Brass Lamp Trick

    Porthole Covers
    Dockside Filters
    Screwed Up Hoses
    Cutting Mats
    Needlenose Fids
    Tongue Depressors Tools
    Vinyl lettering & Designs
    Storage
    Super Honkers
    Stereo Speakers
    Scupper Stains

Chapter Twelve - *Cruising Basics*   115
    Cruise Planning
    Cruising Food
    Entrees
    Jars, Bottles & Cans
    Vegetables
    Beverages

Chapter Thirteen – *Avoiding Mistakes*   123
    Overplanning
    Friends on a Cruise
    Check Engines
    Latest Charts
    Only GPS
    Waiting for Good Weather
    Taking the Dog

Chapter Fourteen - *Cruising The ICW* 133
    The Rules of the Road
    Bridges

Chapter Fifteen - *Observations*   139
    Chicky on the Bow
    Beards
    Filling Up
    No Wake Signs
    Locks

Chapter Sixteen - *Inflatable Dinghies*   151
    Bottom Paint
    Stowing Gear
    Inflatable Floorboards
    Inflating the Inflatable

    Cruising with an Inflatable
    Towing an Inflatable
    The Dinghy at Anchor

    Locking the Dinghy
    Getting Into the Inflatable

Chapter Seventeen – *Safety*   161
    Checking Life Jackets
    Fire Extinguishers

Chapter Eighteen – *Navigation*   171
    Disclaimer
    The Compass
    Cartography

Chapter Nineteen – *Computers*   193
    Electronic Charting Programs
    The Internet
    Search Engines

Chapter Twenty - *Securing Your Boat*   201
    Throttle Ball
    How Propellers Work
    Dockside Connections
    Laundering Lines
    Mooring & Securing a Twin Engine Vessel
    Landing Parallel to the Dock
        No wind
        Wind blowing away from dock
        Wind blowing to dock
        Strong current on bow
    Lassos
    Bowlines & Clove Hitches
    Universal Fenders
    PVC Fender Boards

Chapter Twenty-One – *Mooring*   221
    Mooring Balls
    Anchoring
    Hanging Out in the Bahamas

Chapter Twenty-Two - *The Environment*   229
    Tides, Currents & Wild Words
    Ocean Currents of the World
    Weather
    Single Side Band (SSB)
    Amateur Radio (HAM)
    Learning About Lightning
    Surviving Storms
    The Storm Season

After Forty Years --- Dave Wheeler

Storm Checklist

Chapter Twenty-Three - *Final Thoughts*   267

About the Author   277

After Forty Years --- Dave Wheeler

After Forty Years --- Dave Wheeler

Chapter One
THE BOATS

Very few people know all about boats before they buy one. Most people never plan to get involved with boats. Usually it just happens by accident. Nevertheless, most survive the learning process in spite of disasters, embarrassments and a serious learning process. It often bent the budget badly but passion overcomes reality. In my wildest dreams, I would never have guessed I'd live aboard a boat and survive forty years of "learning experiences", cruising through the Great Lakes, Canada and the Bahamas writing, over 400 articles for marine magazines. The years I spent in the automobile industry helped me buy the boats, while the boats provided the dreams as I worked on cars.

I, like most, started my boat ownership career unexpectedly. Before I met my wife I never thought about boats. *I knew nothing.* I worked at General Motors Styling and automobiles were about the only thing I thought about. Then I met an interesting young lady at GM and we both owned Corvettes. We started going out to lunch together and soon learned we had a lot in

After Forty Years --- Dave Wheeler

common except she was very interested in boats. Her father had a classic, gaff rigged cutter named "Doubloon". He was big on sailing, marine traditions and ships at sea. As time went by, I could see things weren't going to progress unless I knew something about boats. I decided to see what boats were all about. I read books, looked at boats and somewhere along the way, got hooked. Boats were not exactly what I had planned to get into, but they sure were interesting.

I'm not sure how boats took me to the altar but it wasn't long before Jan and I were married. A little later we began looking for a boat. It was a chilly fall day in Michigan when we went out to look at boats. The first little sailboat we saw was a Lightning sailboat, number 4240, an early model made of wood. It was huddled in the back corner of the owner's yard under a heavy canvas cover. Soggy brown leaves almost filled the cockpit and a layer of dust covered everything. Jan and I glanced at each other when the owner said how much he wanted. We didn't say anything, but the price was right and we knew it was our boat. We acted calm and nonchalant as we wrote out the check but when we got in the car we howled with glee and hugged each other. *We had a boat!*

The next morning we went out to look at our new sailboat in the sunlight and learned how little we knew. That boat had aged during the night. The varnish had pale yellow blotches, the canvas on the deck had big bubbles that flexed when we pressed on them and one place on the rail looked as though it had been attacked with an ax. Those scars must have been there the day before but our visions of white sails and summer days wiped out all those ugly details. Now, in the cold light of day, we were reminded that winter was coming, we had some serious work to do and no place to do it.

A newspaper ad led us to one of the local churches. They had a huge heated garage where they kept their Sunday school buses and one stall was for rent. There was plenty of space with heat and light to work on the little sailboat. We could hardly wait to start. It took us most of Saturday to get our tools and gear ready but we were at that garage by sunrise on Sunday morning. Apparently they hadn't expected us so early. There was a big padlock on the door and we learned that the pastor had the only key. It wasn't easy getting an audience with the old gentlemen on a Sunday morning but we finally cornered him and explained the problem. He was appalled. He hadn't realized we were young sinners who would even consider working on Sunday. He made it abundantly clear that the Sabbath was sacred in God's garage, even for small sailboats. That was a serious problem. The weekends were our only free time, which left nights, Saturdays and a few sneak trips on Sunday when the reverend left to tend his flocks.

    I had a little experience with woodwork but we read every boat book we could get our hands on. We worked hard and it wasn't knowledge or skill that made the boat come together. It was sheer enthusiasm. We sanded down the hull but didn't know enough to probe for dry rot. We'd be sorry about that later but we wanted to get some shiny white paint on that boat. Canvas had been glued on the deck and painted, but it was coming off. After some research, we found a material called Hypalon and fastened it to the deck with epoxy. A new name for the boat was in order and, in our optimism, we painted "Project One" on the transom. That was more accurate than we knew. After we added a twelve-volt battery under the foredeck, wired the boat for running lights and made cushions and a cover for the cockpit, we started looking for a marina where we could keep our beautiful sailboat.

    We found just what we wanted on the Clinton River just outside the big fences around Selfridge Air

Force Base. It was time to rent a trailer and take the boat to its new home.

We didn't know zip about trailers and it was some time before we learned how to turn corners and miss curbs at the same time. The only ramp we found wasn't very close to our slip. Some people at the ramp helped us get the boat in the water and it actually floated! Then we realized we didn't have a motor so we had to paddle to our slip.

The Air Base was having their annual air show when we arrived and it was hard to pay strict attention to what we were doing. When the boat was securely tied, it was near the end of the show. Jan and I lifted the long mast upright and sidestepped along awkwardly, trying to keep it in balance. Just then, all the jets came screaming over in the grand finale, assaulting our ears and seeming to be right over the masthead. We almost lost it, dancing back and forth like demented sailors doing the polka with a mast. We finally regained control, slipped the mast into place and fell back on the grass to admire our achievement. That mast stood up there straight and tall, silhouetted against the sky with all the halyards, shrouds and stays taped securely to the mast above the spreaders -- totally out of reach. Well, we did the polka before but now it was time for the two-step.

SAILING LESSONS

On our first days of sailing, we started out downwind as it was the easiest way to go. We'd drink some beer, smooch a little and swat the flies that didn't seem to get blown away, but every time we started back the weather changed. The wind got stronger, water splashed in our faces and the waves seemed bigger. It took us longer to get back to the marina and once we had to fumble our way in at dark. We couldn't understand why that always happened until we invited the most knowledgeable sailor in the marina over for a beer and some advice. When we told him what happened to us, he tried so hard not to laugh he almost choked on his beer. After he regained his composure, he explained very carefully, and with more sensitivity than we deserved, exactly what we had done wrong. We were learning.

We even decided to try the spinnaker that came with the boat. The wind instantly grabbed the sail and the power was frightening. One attempt took me off my feet and came close to turning the boat over. Finally, we got it going right and we started to plane off. Out there on the water without a motor running, the sound of the water burbling in our wake was an experience we've never forgotten. We often sailed after work and even after dark.

Figure 1
The boat that changed my life.

We loved the water but our little sailboat was

pretty slow. Even going to the other side of Lake St. Clair was a big trip and in bad weather staying over in the tiny space below was impossible. At the same time, we became more aware of powerboats zooming by us, heading out of sight to romantic and distant destinations we dared not consider. Maybe it was time for a change even though that little sailboat had taught us to respect the environment, be careful with wood and watch which way the wind is blowing

SWITCHING TO POWER

Things were going well at work but the hours were long and the amount of time we could spend on the boat was limited. At our speed, we couldn't get very far and I was jealous of the guys with those powerboats that flew by us. I spent the winter selling the idea to Jan and early the next spring we put up a "for sale" sign. I don't know if it was the fresh paint or our handiwork, but it was sold in a week. The guy bought our boat, our slip, our lines and we were without a boat at the beginning of the summer. We immediately started some serious shopping but those little powerboats were way more expensive than we thought.

Finally, the great day came and we got our powerboat. It was a 28 foot, Tollycraft sport fisherman with twin Chrysler gasoline engines. It did almost forty miles an hour and after all that slow sailing we could go anyplace... *anyplace!* We may have been traitors to our sailing friends but forty miles an hour was great. We decided to head up to Lake Huron and visit the cottage that Jan's folks had built at Port Sanilac. It was about a hundred miles away but, not to worry, it was only two and a half hours at our new speed. We went up there one morning and came back the same night. We learned some

After Forty Years --- Dave Wheeler

things. That kind of speed sucked up fuel like crazy and we were exhausted after five hours of running all out in lumpy water.

Nevertheless, we could travel and explore. The world was ours. The first cruises are the best ones, or maybe we just remember them as the best. They were totally carefree days and we never worried about a thing. We knew that nothing could possibly happen to us and, for a while, it didn't. As time went by we began to learn it was actually possible to have something break. It was an education we hadn't expected and every year we learned about more things that could go wrong. Each year our checklists got longer as we found out about things that should be checked, most of which were brought to our attention the hard way.

There are all kinds of beginners and dreamers and, in the beginning, many of us sail on without concern. The force of our new dream entrances us and we don't see outside of our minds. It isn't all turquoise seas under tropical skies, but we never think about ugly things like tall ships encrusted with ice, sailors with frozen hands trying to climb the rigging, or a fire aboard. All boat owners, no matter how old or grizzled they may be, are romantics at heart. I understand those dreams and, invariably, see the wonders before I see the realities. A new idea, a beautiful vision, or the first taste of a delicious wine stays in the mind long after the knowledge that intoxication can be followed by illness. That first wild flush of enthusiasm can be dangerous. We were lucky we learned in small pieces and in payments we could afford. Now we have schemes, systems and strategies. Sometimes we're so busy working out schedules that we miss some of the scenery or neglect to smell the roses, but maybe that's the way it has to be.

DINGHIES

We decided we needed a dinghy to use while anchored, or perhaps just to enjoy cruising around. This turned out to be a more expensive project than anticipated. We bought a small fiberglass dinghy with a six horse outboard on it. We soon learned that the bottom of a dinghy left in saltwater for a while, quickly becomes home to an incredible collection of sea life. The obvious solution was to install davits and a power lift, which put the swim platform nearly underwater with the dinghy up. Now trim tabs were necessary to lift the stern of the boat when we were running. That wasn't all. It would cost us more later. My daughter wanted to use the dinghy by herself and I kept telling her she wasn't old enough yet. Somewhere along the line, she became convinced that I had promised to buy her a Whaler when she turned sixteen. That misunderstanding cost me dearly.

THE 38-FOOT EGG HARBOR

Everybody gets the "bigger boat" urge and we were no exception. Egg Harbor boats had a great reputation and a seagoing look. We hung around the local showroom until they made us an offer we couldn't refuse. The boat was a 38 ft. Egg Harbor sport fisherman, ten feet longer than our Tollycraft. That may not sound like much but it was over one third longer and it looked enormous to us.

We did do a good thing by tying the Tollycraft alongside the Egg Harbor and just handing the stuff over to the new boat. We did a bad thing by not selling the Tollycraft first and wound up making payments and paying for storage of both boats all winter. That was a lesson we will never forget. We named the new boat

"Halcyon" and had a little plaque made, describing the mythical bird that built its nest on the open seas, about the time of the winter solstice and had the power to calm the wind and waves.

Figure 2
38-foot Egg Harbor

It took time before Jan and I were working together. At first we ran into each other a lot and sometimes even spoke harshly to each other. Eventually, we worked out who's going where, when and with which line. A little practice can avoid embarrassment and damage. There was a municipal marina on Lake St. Clair where we went on Tuesday mornings to practice docking the boat.

On a trip down from Tobermory on the Canadian side of Lake Huron, we docked at a new place called Bayfield. That was a mistake and we learned to evaluate marinas much more carefully. The docks were weak and swayed as we landed. The pilings were skinny and the planks had sharp edges. Then we heard a weather forecast for severe storms later that night. Around 4:30 we decided to head across Lake Huron to Port Sanilac where they had a more protected harbor and substantial docks. It was 41 miles across at that point but we could make that in a couple of hours. It was getting dark when we arrived and we barely got the boat tied up before the storm hit. A sailboat arrived in the middle of the storm. They were having a problem getting the sails down in the heavy winds and the mainsail was flying straight out horizontally. The dockmaster decided he would help them and turned on a powerful spotlight so they could see. Actually he blinded them, and after a dreadful struggle, they dropped the anchor in the middle of the harbor. That spotlight burned a picture into our memory. We were thankful we had started earlier.

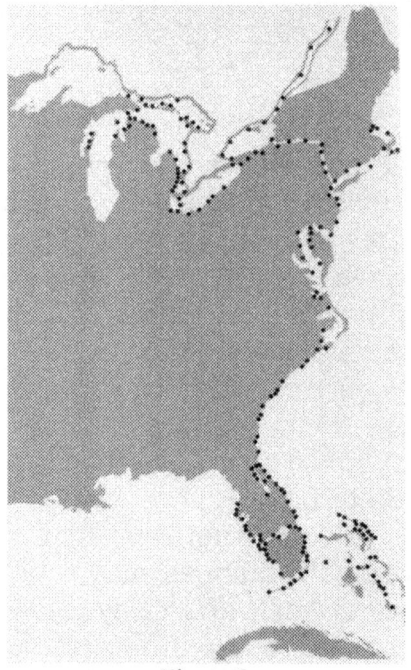

Figure 3
Our Ports of Call Map

On an early cruise with the 38 Egg, we saw a

small freighter with a map of the Great Lakes on the front of his fly bridge with dots showing all the ports he regularly serviced. We thought it would be a great idea to have a map on our fly bridge with dots for all the harbors we visited. We were proud of that map and it started a lot of conversations. It also encouraged us to try new harbors, rather than those we had already visited.

41-FOOT EGG HARBOR MOTORYACHT

We soon wanted an even bigger boat and purchased a used 41 foot Egg Harbor Motor Yacht. The price was right but it needed work. The boat was up and covered for the winter when we bought it, so every weekend that winter was spent working on it. I'd take my lunch and a heater with me and work all day. I scraped out the bilges and painted the wood down there with green wood preservative. I also refinished the interior wood, tuned up the engines, put in new carpets, installed a new aft deck enclosure and rebuilt some of the furniture. Friends were with us when we took the boat across Lake St. Clair. The weather turned out rougher than forecast and the round bottom Egg rolled a lot. Drinks on the helm hit the floor and my friend's wife got seasick on the new carpet. I had obviously not learned enough about guests on board.

On our next trip, we decided to go up through Lake Huron to Lake Superior. The marina mechanic checked the engines and running gear before we left. On the St. Clair River at Sarnia, we heard some unusual sounds and then smelled hot metal. Foolishly, I lifted up the engine hatch to see what was going on down there. *That was the wrong move.* It let more air into the engine room and flames shot up. I slammed down the hatch and turned into the channel to the Sarnia Marina, as smoke started coming out of the engine room exhausts. It was vapor from the automatic fire extinguisher, which put out the fire, but shut down the engines for lack of air.

We were adrift in a busy channel, trying to decide if we should put life preservers on our daughter and the dog and throw them overboard, when a Canadian boat pulled alongside. He asked if I wanted a tow and before I answered he added, "I have a bridle", which made the choice an easy one. If he knew about bridles, he probably knew something about towing. He brought us right in alongside a dock which we later realized was the fuel dock but had no way to move. I cautiously checked below again. The fire was out but one of the transmissions was still glowing cherry red. Every piece of insulation and anything that wasn't metal was gone. We learned later that before we left, the mechanic had aligned the engines and shafts, but on that side they had not bolted one engine back down. The engine got out of line and created heat in the transmission that resulted in the fire.

Grandma and Grandpa took the dog and our daughter, while we spent our vacation with the boat hanging in the slings. The yard made the repairs but vacation time was gone and we never did get to Lake Superior. After that experience we were never comfortable with the boat. We kept listening for trouble and looking for another boat.

43-VIKING DOUBLE CABIN

We traded in the Egg for a new 43 Viking. We visited the yard at New Gretna, took pictures of the boat being built and talked them into taking a complete set of photos during the construction. The photos showed where every wire and pipe was, which was invaluable when working on the boat or installing new equipment.

We took the boat to Florida before I retired, stored it at a marina in Melbourne and started on a cruising program that worked out well for us. I would save up vacation time, include any possible weekends or holidays, maybe cheat a little. I'd make the plans and plot out all the courses long before it was time to go. About a week beforehand, Jan would take our daughter and depart with the car to provision the boat. I would then fly in and we'd leave on our planned cruise.

Figure 4
Our 43-foot Viking

50-FOOT OCEAN ALEXANDER

We had been talking about retiring and buying a larger boat, perhaps a trawler with more room and less costly to operate, when an Ocean Alexander docked across from us. The owner was a dealer and invited us aboard. The interior was absolutely superb. We liked the trawler but it was a little smaller than our boat. The dealer showed us some brochures of their fifty foot Mark

1. Although it was exactly what we wanted, the price was more than we could handle, but now we knew what we were looking for.

We found an ad for a 50 foot Ocean Alexander at a New England dealership, owned by the former America's Cup skipper, Ted Hood. We looked at the boat and made a silly offer. Mr. Hood took the offer and since he was the Ocean Alexander dealer, we had new boat warranties on everything.

Figure 5
Our 50-foot Ocean Alexander

We agreed to buy the Ocean Alexander and outfitted it exactly as we wanted, but one problem remained. We still had to sell the Viking because we had learned the agonies of supporting two boats. Finally, we were free to leave and cruise around New England before heading to Florida but we couldn't seem to get on our way. The harbor at Marblehead had a bar that could be passed only at high tide. The first morning that the tide was predicted to be high enough, I got up early and looked out a porthole. Either I had gone blind or somebody had painted the outside of the port light with white paint. That was when I learned about New England fog. A few days later it had thinned out a bit and we set out for Provincetown with radar and new Loran. My first mate and I had a routine for handling our boats and were sure we knew exactly what each of us had to do. However, the Ocean Alexander was bigger, fatter and required more encouragement to bring the long keel around. Docking that boat for the first time was interesting. We only ran into each other once, or maybe twice.

    We also left Provincetown in a light fog. I was concentrating on using the new instruments and didn't check the tides and currents. We arrived at the bridge midway through the Cape Cod Canal and suddenly learned there was a fearsome current. At the end of the Canal there was a solid wall of fog over Buzzard's Bay, so we turned right to spend the night at Onset Bay. The next morning we headed for Martha's Vineyard, where the current at Wood's Hole had the buoy laid over on its side. That was the last time I messed with Mother Nature. Now I get up in the middle of the night, if necessary, to check tides and currents.

    This first section illustrates how many things we learned through experience, but it was obvious we needed to learn far more. Therefore, we joined the United Sates Power Squadron and eventually took every course they offered. In the process, I became a Squadron Commander and worked in the District and National organizations. Jan and I were rather unhappy about the USPS refusal to let women be independent members, so we joined the local Flotilla of the United States Coast Guard Auxiliary, where women were not only members, but officers. Again we wound up taking all the Coast Guard courses and I became a Flotilla Commander. The knowledge acquired from both organizations has come to our aid time and time again. I heartily advise anyone interested in boats to, at least, take the basic boating courses both organizations offer.

Chapter Two

MAINTENANCE

It may not always be fun, but it is rather important to keep the boat afloat. Anyone who spends enough time aboard eventually gets lessons in plumbing, painting, varnishing, woodworking, engine maintenance and electrical repairs, whether they want to or not. You simply can't survive without good maintenance. You may have all the charts, computers, GPS and navigation programs but if the boat doesn't work, you're in trouble and you could lose both the boat and your life.

CRUISING RELIGION

This was an article I wrote for fun but there's a bit of truth here that shouldn't be ignored and these are important ceremonies that must never be neglected.

Yea, every morning before leaving the dock I must go down to the temple of the engines and the generator, get down on my knees and perform the morning rites, anointing these machines with oils of Rotella and quenching their thirsts. I visit this shrine

After Forty Years --- Dave Wheeler

once every hour as we cross the Gulf Stream, seeking confirmation of our supplications. Occasionally, we must make offerings of filters, hoses or impellers before leaving.

When I have failed to keep the faith, overlooked some part of the rituals or did not study my catechisms properly, I seek forgiveness. I must call a mechanic and confess my sins. He will then speak to the gods of the engine room, and when they are appeased, he will require that I make an offering, testing my faith and my account at the bank. The size of that offering depends on how sinful I have been. This, of course, is in addition to regular tithes for dockage and boat payments.

To avoid future sin, we frequent the classes of the United States Power Squadron, hearing the words they preach from the sacred writings of Chapman and Maloney. Searching for the truth, we listen to the doctrines of advanced piloting and navigation. We were enlightened by the words of Bowditch and Dutton. Our zeal was great, we persevered and we were rewarded with stars and bars. We were encouraged to go forth on the waters and spread the word of the squadrons.

Now I have atoned for past sins and learned the words of those who have overcome the power of the seas. My faith is strong and I can face the devils of navigation, invoking the powers of the omnipotent Global Positioning System above us. False witnesses no longer distort the messages I receive. I know that someday there will be even greater truths unsullied by those who would deceive us.

I shall be able to sail through the valleys of great seas and fear no evil. Thy chart plotter and thy radar comfort me. I shall avoid the excesses of great speed on the waterway, rocking the sailors in their traditional sackcloths. I shall listen to the priests of the National Weather Service. Above all, I will eschew conceit in my recent learning and wait for calm seas, lest I be baptized by foaming green waters or swallowed by a great whale. I will plot my courses on a chart and ignore those hypercritical mockers who depend solely on the coordinates from above. I shall prepare my vessel with food and water or I will fast at anchor while I review my sins. Upon our return to this land of milk and honey, I shall patiently wait at the pearly gates of the designated marina for the blessing of customs, declaring our purity.

So sayeth this poor prophet, the recipient of great revelations and visions. One who prays that you may all enjoy clear waters and blue skies. Know ye all that cruising confidence requires great faith. Now is the time to get serious.

THE ENGINE ROOM

Engines are the most expensive piece of equipment on your boat and they deserve a lot of attention. If the engine room is a miserable, hot, uncomfortable place, you may not want to stay down there long enough to give those machines the proper amount of time and attention.

The floorboards in many engine rooms are made of stamped aluminum with ugly little bumps that tear up your knees if you spend any time crawling around down there. Scrap carpet might be OK but the outdoor type is better. No matter how careful you are, a few drops of something will get on the carpet and it will gradually get imbedded with oil and diesel grime. Outdoor carpet will survive scrubbing and hosing on the dock much better. When you look for carpeting, take a cigarette lighter with you. Ask for a tiny piece, take it outside and see if you can make it burn. In a twin engine arrangement, a box seat covered with the same carpet, located between the engines, will give you a comfortable place to work and a storage spot for oil or tools. It may sound a bit strange, but I fondle my engines. I feel every hose connection and if my hand comes away wet, I know I'd better check the hose clamps. Your friends may be impressed with your handsomely carpeted engine room, but the real reason to put carpet down there is to make it a better workplace. I have white fiberglass engine pans and I clean them every morning when we're cruising. That way I can see any drips, where they are and what color they are. Black is oil, diesel fuel is almost clear, the engine water is slightly brown from the additive we put in it and transmission fluid is pink.

Heat in the engine room is a problem while you're cruising. We wait until the next morning when it's cooler to check the engines before we leave. We've also installed a big window fan in one end of the engine room. There is no window, but that big fan moves the air anyhow. A friend has an air conditioning duct that can divert air down there, which is certainly a good option.

Lighting is important. If you can't see clearly, you can miss something. We first used 12V fluorescent lights from an RV store and they did a good job. Then we changed to 110V fluorescent lights that really light up the world below decks. The tubes should be supported or enclosed for safety. All the associated 110V wiring for the lighting and large window fan is safely tucked in the overhead.

THE GENERATOR

We have a big old generator with a famous name but no available parts or service. The company moved out of the country and the pirates who still own some parts are just waiting for people to call them. Our

After Forty Years --- Dave Wheeler

generator was in the boat we bought so we had no choice, as is the case with most people. It was a big old ugly machine with a difficult to access door. The generator needs to be checked the same as the engine; fluid levels, hose connections and the pan below it. Regular maintenance requires taking the door off quite often and if you're cruising, you should check inside every morning. After awhile the holes get so distorted that the fasteners won't stay in. Eventually even self-tapping screws enlarge the holes and start falling out. I've gone through two levels of larger screws and still have some problems. In addition, the so-called stainless screws rust and frequently need replaced.

Eventually I replaced the heavy steel door with a stiff aluminum panel about 1/16th of an inch thick. Aluminum is much lighter and doesn't require such heavy-duty fastenings. Velcro strips between the panel and the generator housing hold it firmly in place. Two pieces of aluminum in a J shape are screwed fast to the base of the generator and help support the weight of the door panel. It helps position the door and I can just pull the panel loose at the top for a quick check. To take it off, I squeeze my fingers behind the panel at the top and it comes loose easily. That works better than the handles I first put on it. The old insulation was torn up and thick with oil and grunge, so I took it off and glued new insulation of the same size and type to the aluminum. Even with the insulation, the new aluminum piece is light enough to move it out of the way with one hand when I have work to do on the generator.

Almost every new visitor to the Bahamas thinks anchoring is free, but that's another one of those boating illusions that soon fade away. The power to run a refrigerator, charge your batteries or keep the freezer cold has to come from someplace, and for most people, that's a generator. Unfortunately, when it gets around to serious anchor time, most boats have generators that are far too big. They may have seemed like a good thing when you bought the boat, but it just isn't a good thing for cruising and being at anchor. It soon becomes apparent out at anchor that it takes fuel to make watts, and at current prices in the Bahamas, it may cost you more for just hanging around out there than you thought. Dockage prices in the islands may appear to be lower than the cost of running the generator, but there's a catch. Most of the islands have to run generators too, so when you add their separate water and electricity charges, you may not want to head for the docks right away.

CHANGING FILTERS

My filters are Racors but the basics are the same for most fuel filters. I smell like diesel fuel for the rest of the day after changing the filters, but I don't mind when I remember a long day in the Gulf of Mexico with one engine out and the other one skipping a beat now and then. After that trip, my filters get new filter elements regularly, and if I'm starting a long trip of any kind, they get changed again, whether it's the scheduled time or not.

I prefer Racor filter elements but that's just my own opinion. I once spent a day in a taxi looking for filters in a strange harbor. (I know I should have plenty of spares, but I goofed.) It wasn't a total loss because I found several different brands of filter elements that will also work in my Racor filter/separator units. Automotive shops that specialize in truck parts are an excellent source of filters.

Here's how I change my filters, step by step. First, I get all the equipment together and checked out before getting in the engine room: laundry soap bottle for the dirty fuel, the bottom half of a plastic milk bottle to put under the filters when I drain them, a standard yellow jug of clean diesel fuel and a pail with a plastic bag inside for the dirty filters and miscellaneous trash. I also use a clean, outboard fuel line with a squeeze bulb, flushed with diesel fuel, to pump fresh diesel fuel into the filters.

Then I open all the filter boxes or plastic bags and make sure all the parts, pieces and O rings are there. I shut off the fuel valves going from the fuel tanks to the filter/separators and then, with the half milk bottle under the filters, I open the small valve at the bottom of the plastic bowl. This releases some of the dirty fuel and, with the container below in the right position, I unscrew the top of the Racor unit and let all the old fuel in the unit run out. I wet the new seal with diesel fuel before replacing the old one inside the top. There is a small O ring on the T screw that closes down the top of the filter unit, which should also be wet with clean diesel fuel before it's put on the T screw. After cleaning out the units by running clean fuel into them, I pour the dirty fuel into the empty soap bottle. Then I move the pail with the plastic bag close, lift out the filter insert and drop it right in the pail without spilling a drop.

Next, I move the container of clean diesel fuel up to the filter. Squeezing hard on the fuel line squeeze bulb, I hose off the centrifuge and the inside of the bowl with diesel fuel, allowing the dirty fuel to run out into the waste container. After the new filter element is put in, I completely fill the Racor unit to the top, again using the fuel hose and screw on the top. Some fuel may be forced out as you screw down the top but it's easily wiped up with paper towels. If the fuel is right to the top there isn't any room for air. (Air is not a healthy thing for diesel fuel systems.)

The last step is important. *Open the valves*

between the fuel tank and the filter again. I've forgotten to do that and it's embarrassing after you leave the dock, wave good-bye and an engine stalls out. I know from experience that if I head down to the engine room immediately when the engine falters and open the fuel valves, there is often enough fuel in the system to restart the engines. On one occasion, I managed to run all the fuel out of an engine, which is bad news because it's a long process to get the fuel flowing again.

My engines are Lehman Fords and, although you may have another make, the basic process of starting an engine after it runs out of fuel is the same. Your engine manual will show you exactly where to find the things I'm going to describe. Close the main fuel valves while you take the top off the Racor unit and make sure it is completely full. If necessary, add more fuel and replace the top. Open the main fuel valves again and loosen the fuel bleed screws on the top of the secondary fuel filters while pumping the fuel lift pump. My lift pump is manual and the lever has to be operated through the full arc or it doesn't pump fuel. Eventually, after your thumb is pretty sore, air and fuel will bubble out around both fuel bleed screws. The final move is to undo the bleed screws on the side of the fuel injection pump and work the fuel lift pump again until all the air there is expelled by fuel. Then I go topside, cross my fingers, start the engines and tell myself I'll *never* forget to open the fuel valves again.

SEACOCKS

Most seacocks are opened by first turning a releasing key, or wing nut, on one side and then using a handle on the other side to open it. Handles vary from rods a quarter inch in diameter to flat handles about a quarter inch thick and maybe three quarters wide. In either case, it isn't easy to get a good grip on them and it hurts your hand if the seacock requires some effort to open or close. We put a six-inch piece of PVC over the smaller handles, which makes them much easier to turn. If it doesn't want to cooperate, don't force it. Shoot WD-40 in there and wait a while longer.

The best practice is to have the seacocks properly cleaned when the boat is out of the water but we sometimes forget to do that.

Wing nuts are hard to reach and difficult to get a good grip on. We made a key from a 1 1/2" square piece of teak about six inches long. It has a slot in one end for the wing nut and a dowel through the other end to give us a grip. We use wood for these instead of metal because it's easier on bronze or plastic. Wing nuts are used on many marine devices such as strainers, portholes, hatch fasteners, valves and plumbing. The key is a great help but be careful not to break anything, as it can apply much more pressure than turning by hand.

A DOUBLE BASE FOR PUMPS

At one time we had a water pump in the engine room that had to be removed often to change the diaphragms. It was screwed fast to the engine room floor and, after removing it several times, the screw holes became enlarged and the screws wouldn't hold. I made a base of 1/2 inch plywood with four machine screws standing up through the plywood. Holes for those screws were drilled slightly smaller than the machine screws so they had to be screwed into the wood. The countersink heads were also glued into the bottom with epoxy. Just inside of the machine screws, I used four, heavy, self-tapping screws to fasten the base to the engine room floor permanently.

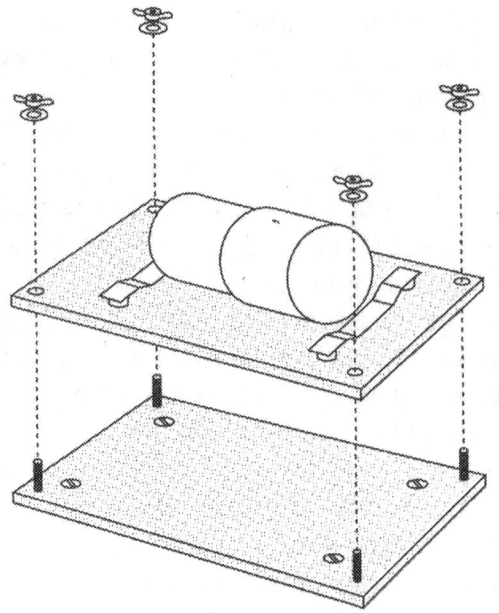

Figure 6

Equipment like pumps must be removed and repaired occasionally. The screw holes holding the base enlarge and will no longer hold. The problem is solved by using two bases, one permanently fastened and the other with bolts and wing nuts.

A second base had the pump screwed fast to it. The corners of the second base had four holes drilled to accept the upstanding machine screws. The second pump base is held down with four wing nuts and lock washers. Now the pump and its base can be removed without damaging the engine room floor. Since then, I've found that this double base arrangement works well for other devices that have to be removed now and then.

Chapter Three
ELECTRICAL

110V WIRING

As more electrical and electronic devices become available, the amount of wiring in boats continues to increase. Considering the spaces and shapes that result as a boat is built, wiring is often in places that are difficult to reach.

One solution to the problem is attaching new wires to the old ones and using the old wires to pull the good ones through. Properly crimped connectors on the wire, plus shrink tubing, can hold the old and new wires together, even in tight spots. Liquid soap or talcum can help the wires slide through the tight spaces. A silicone gel might help but read the label to make sure it has no petroleum content that could damage the insulation.

When a wire has to be installed in a new area, a slightly stiffer lead wire, a light plumbing snake, or a heavy piece of clear nylon fishline can be used as a pull wire. It takes two to do the "wiring Tango." One person gets the lead wire started through and the other person looks for the end. This may not be easy, sometimes communications are difficult and a bit of shouting results. Once contact is made, the new wire can be pulled through and attached.

THE CONNECTIONS

Most people have one of those standard plastic boxes of connectors and terminals, plus a crimping tool of some sort. Crimps with those old tools can come loose because it's difficult to apply enough pressure to make them foolproof.

Some people put their faith in solder but the ABYC (American Boat and Yacht Council) standards say "a good solder joint should not be the sole means of mechanical connection in a circuit." A reliable soldered joint is not as easy as it appears. It depends on getting just the right amount of heat to the various metals involved. Bad solder joints may not be evident. The wire and the terminal have to be free of corrosion. In a good joint, properly heated solder will "wick" into the wires. The correct solder is 40% lead and 60% tin and it should have a rosin core, instead of an acid core. The finished joint should be bright and shiny and have a minimum amount of solder. There is also some peril in using a hot soldering iron in tight quarters and a torch can be very dangerous.

There are better crimpers that make more dependable crimps. The jaws have a little stud inside, opposite the recess, for the connector. Rotate the connector so the stud is not on the side with the crack in the metal barrel inside the connector. The stud compresses one side of the connector right into the other

Figure 7
Professionals use crimps with a stud that creates a depression inside the connector, insuring a solid connection.

side and the manufacturer says the pressure actually fuses the metal of the wire to the metal of the connector. If you really want to be positive about a crimp, there are ratcheting crimpers that won't release unless you have put enough pressure on the connector.

Marine grade adhesive-lined shrink tubing will provide protection and strength for wire connections. A heat gun makes them shrink tightly around a joint and the melting adhesive adheres the tubing to both the wire and the insulation, making it air and watertight. Once shrunk, the tubing can tolerate a wide range of hot or cold temperatures. White shrink tubing is available for identifying wires at the same time connections are being made.

SURGE PROTECTORS

Many things fail to get your attention until there's a problem. We never heard of surge protectors until disaster struck one day in the out islands. We had come

After Forty Years --- Dave Wheeler

into a marina to fill our water tanks, make some ice cubes, watch one of our VCR tapes and enjoy a little A/C that night. Snugly plugged in, we were cozy and cool, when everything went "whunk" and our world went dark -- no power, no A/C, no joy. It didn't last too long and it came back on with a bang, but the TV didn't come back on and we could smell some hot Bakelite. We fiddled around with the TV for a while but it didn't respond at all. Finally, we gave up and went to bed. The next morning, Jan popped some good breakfast stuff in the microwave but it didn't wave back. It had gone to visit the great electrician in the sky.

We had been zapped by a large power surge. The generators on the island had gone down and, after repairs were made, they came back on line with a sudden and enormous surge in electrical power that destroyed our TV and microwave. The only good thing was that we were on our way back to the U.S. where we could get our appliances repaired, or at the worst, replaced. Our local expert made "tsk" and "hm-m-m" noises as he looked inside the TV and the microwave. He asked if we had surge protectors and that's when we got the electrical lecture.

Electrical power is a major problem for many marinas. Boats want electrical power when they arrive at a marina and demand a lot of it. Larger boats with multiple air conditioning units are heavy hitters on the power supply. Under some circumstances, outside the boat, even outside the marina, can send spikes, or sudden increases of voltage, through the electrical system. A big boat can create its own damage by switching on water heaters, refrigerators or air conditioning at the same time. Surge protectors can't completely eliminate a powerful surge and voltage surges induced by lightning are far more powerful than these devices can accommodate. If lightning strikes another boat or an adjacent facility, it may reduce a surge in the incoming power.

The prime component in a surge protector is a metal oxide varister. It's made of compressed powdered material similar to those in diodes. MOVs are a composite consisting of grains of one material, with another material between them. The grains are conductive, but the material between them is insulation that breaks down when excessive voltage is applied. The price depends on the amount and type of MOV in the surge protector. To maximize surge protection, choose the highest surge energy rating you can afford. Each time a powerful surge comes through the protector, the insulating material between the grains breaks down. Surge protectors degrade if they see repeated and powerful currents. Some surge current will still get through an MOV. They are not perfect, but physically large MOV's (diameter) can cut this "leak-through" current in half or more. Eventually, they will lose their ability to protect. On earlier models you couldn't tell when they were sick or tired but many of the present models have an LED that lights up if they're still functional.

There are many surge protectors available, from those with no guarantees, to expensive devices like those made for industrial operations or companies with sensitive equipment like computers or electronics. I was impressed with a catalog that guaranteed to replace up to $10,000.00 of my equipment damaged by an electrical surge while properly connected to their surge protectors. Unfortunately, there was also a long statement about the conditions of that guarantee. It said that the surge protector must be plugged in to a properly wired and grounded AC outlet and no extension cords, adapters or other ground wires can be used. The "building" (think marina) must comply with all local electrical codes. A transient vessel in a strange marina would have a tough time proving that all the electrical power was properly delivered. It makes sense that all guarantees are off if you have homemade wiring connections or extensions on the boat. Nevertheless, I bought three. I figured that if they're willing to write out a guarantee, the product must be somewhat defensible.

ELECTRICAL DISTRIBUTION

People get in trouble by not properly distributing incoming electrical power.

Many larger boats have 220V power. Captains or owners sometimes think that with two-twenty, they have all the power they'll ever need and it's an ugly surprise when the A/C goes down. 220V is usually divided into two 110V systems. Power should be distributed between them based on the total amperage the appliances use. Every appliance or air conditioning unit has the required amperage printed someplace on it. In a simplistic approach, adding up those numbers and dividing by two will tell you how much to put on each side. For example, here is a list of electrical needs for each 110V side on a large boat.

Side A: washer/dryer, outlets for coffee maker, computer, fans, hairdryer, ice maker, TV & VCR, toaster oven, salon A/C, master stateroom A/C, freezer & battery charger.

Side B: refrigerator & microwave, water heater, V berth A/C, pilot house A/C.

Splitting the amperage in half may need to be modified by the power and importance of some items. For example, some combinations will shut down the breakers more often, so the freezer, may merit extra protection. It's easy to see how putting just one of these services on the wrong side can wreak havoc. It's best to check out all the amperage requirements carefully.

MONITORING

If we have to leave our boat for a while, we have an inexpensive way to learn if the electrical power has been off while we were gone. We set an electric clock with the right time when we leave and if the clock has fallen behind when we get back, we know the power has been off. Further, we can determine exactly how long the power was off by the difference in the time it shows.

12 VOLT POWER

I had trouble topping off my 8D batteries. At first I tried carefully pouring the distilled water in those little holes, which was a disaster. Then a friend of mine suggested using a dish soap bottle with a push-pull top. You pull it out to pour and then push it in to stop the flow. I cleaned the bottles out thoroughly, because soap in the battery didn't sound like a good idea. After filling the bottle with distilled water, I held the top over the opening and pulled up on the bottle. When I wanted to stop the flow, I simply pushed the bottle down against the edge of the battery opening. It worked like a charm but a container made for the job is better. You fill it with distilled water and open it when you put the spout in the battery opening. When the water reaches the spout, it automatically shuts off. 8D batteries are heavy and they do have to be replaced after a while. The architects of my boat decided to put the batteries in a corner of the engine room, almost enclosed, to keep them away from the engine room heat,

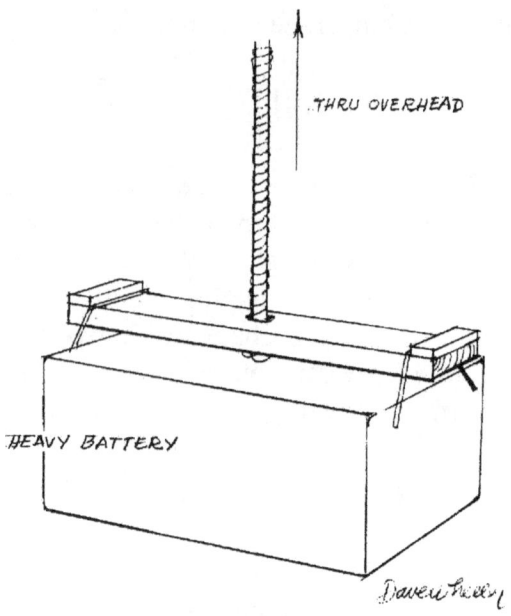

Figure 8

8D batteries are heavy and difficult to move in the confines of an engine room. We used this handle to lift the batteries with an attached line going through the overhead.

which makes them nearly inaccessible. Lying on my stomach, reaching in there and getting enough purchase to lift them out of the battery boxes was nearly impossible. I called some pros and they sent two young fellows, who crawled in there and lifted the batteries out. Nevertheless, it would still be a problem for me, so I came up with the following system. I made a handle of solid 2x4 that was a bit longer than the batteries. The 2x4 had small cross pieces on each end so the built in battery handles would fit over the ends and not slide off. There was also a one-inch hole in the center of the 2x4 for the end of a heavy nylon line. On each side of the salon, the carpet was peeled back and a one-inch hole was drilled through the floor. (It's a good idea to make sure where it's coming through in the engine room.) One end of a nylon line was dropped down the hole in the floor and then put through the hole in the 2x4 and locked with a stopper knot. The next time the batteries had to be changed, I had two friends help me. The strongest one stayed above and lifted the batteries with the line and the other one in the engine room moved the batteries horizontally out of the battery box. From there it was a piece of cake, more or less.

    I avoided gel batteries that never have to be filled. My expert friends couldn't agree whether that was a good thing. Some said they always wanted to be able to see inside the battery so they knew exactly what was going on. Then, there was some publicity about the gel battery warranty not covering a variance in the charging voltage. That put me off for some time but recently I decided to buy completely sealed truck batteries. I bought them with some trepidation but they were installed on 18 February, 2000 and have performed well so far.

After Forty Years --- Dave Wheeler

Chapter Four

VARNISH & PAINT

VARNISHING TEAK

Boats generate illusions. People tell me that living on a boat is not expensive and the maintenance is easier than mowing lawns. There's also a constantly recurring idea that someone will invent a new teak finish that lasts forever. Imported boats have brought tons of teak to this country because it's so cheap and plentiful in the Orient. Boats made in this country have kept pace by increasing their use of teak. No other wood is quite like it. It's truly beautiful and it's one of the few woods resistant to rot.

On the exterior, teak is used for doors, window and door frames, moldings and decks. Teak finishes exposed to the sun have to be faithfully maintained. The alternative is taking the finish down to the wood and starting over which can be a major task. On the interior there's solid wood in frames, handles, moldings and the inside of doors. These are usually finished with a rubbed effect, varnish or oil. Matte finishes will not stand up in

After Forty Years --- Dave Wheeler

sunlight. Few people seem to realize that when the sun shines in windows and portholes, the finish inside can be damaged, and when doors are open, the inside matte finish is in the sun. Matte finishes on interior handrails will soon shine, as your hands polish the surface with use. Handrails and the inside of window frames will look better and last longer with gloss varnish.

On the interior, many surfaces are covered with veneer. Out of the sun it may seem indestructible, but it's subject to staining from grease, body oils or spills. Many people use teak oil inside, but if the veneer is always out of the sun, a matte finish will give the wood the best protection because it seals the surface better than oil. A water leak can make that thin layer of wood lift away from the surface and it's almost impossible to glue it back in place without leaving some indications of the repair. A dent or a gouge in veneer is extremely difficult to repair because the veneer thickness is only 1/28th of an inch. In most cases, an entirely new section of veneer is required because piecing it will show. We know one captain who framed a nice picture and hung it permanently over a stained area.

The best finishes start from bare wood, which requires removing the present finish. Paint and varnish removers are messy and will damage other finishes or materials if drips are not caught on a drop cloth or instantly removed.

Heat guns and scrapers can do a good job used in combination. On a molding or a rail, if you're right handed, hold the heat gun in your left hand and heat up the old varnish as you work to your left. Once you get the swing of it, the scraper in your right hand follows along, taking off the hottest varnish ,as your left hand heats the next section with the gun. When the varnish is ready to be scraped off it will discolor a bit and start to bubble up. Be careful not to overheat the wood. It can blacken and actually char. A heat gun can also damage fiberglass and other materials close by.

Once the finish is removed, smoothing and sanding the wood is next. Power hand sanders are okay for the initial surfacing. Wet or dry sandpaper is best for the final sanding by hand. I start with 240 grit and finish it off with 150. It cuts best if it's rinsed with water often and kept clean. It doesn't make a lot of uncontrolled dust and wetting the wood brings up grain fibers, as well as revealing areas where some finish remains. A sheet of sandpaper cut in quarters will almost wrap around a piece of 1x2. Using a sanding block helps make the surface level.

Professional cabinetmakers use flat square pieces of steel as scrapers to obtain the final surface. Expert woodworkers can make a smoother surface with a scraper than most of us do with a sander. Most people use the regular scrapers from a hardware store or marine catalog. *Be very careful with scrapers.* A wrong move can put an ugly gouge in the surface. A scraper should be sharp as the proverbial razor and, if they are not held at exactly the right angle, they'll peel off a fine ribbon of wood. It's a marvelous tool, but practice first on something not critical.

Varnishes vary in their ability to resist UV rays from the sun. Check the label for the UV resistance. Varnishes can be formulated for different characteristics, such as easy brushing, spraying, fast or slow drying time and durability. They may have combinations of Tung, linseed or soy oil, or resins such as alkyds, urethanes and phenols. Two part clear finishes will last much longer and give you a magnificent surface but they take more work to apply properly. They are also more difficult to remove or touch up. I have had difficulty mixing the right amount for the job with the two part finishes and often wind up with half a can of very hard varnish. Many

After Forty Years --- Dave Wheeler

companies seem to be moving in the direction of one part polyurethane in both paints and varnishes. A high quality spar varnish with maximum UV protection is easy to repair and will maintain an excellent appearance if new coats are added regularly.

When varnishing, pick the best day you can. Wind and dust can create problems. A friend of ours takes his boat out in the bay to put on the final coats of varnish. Rain showers can be a disaster and, in many areas, heat and humidity are constant. Tape is the first order of business. Good tape jobs will save time and you can concentrate on flowing out the varnish. Brushing carefully around the edges of things takes a few extra minutes, while the last varnish you put on gets sticky. On a long hot job in the summer sun, 3M's #225 silver masking tape holds up longest. We use their blue #2090 tape for most projects. We get the tape off as soon as possible, even though 3M rates the silver tape for 30 days and the blue tape for 7 days. The prices reflect about the same ratio. If you need an exact edge, the #256 green tape does a perfect job but it leaves behind a sticky residue if left on very long. Make sure tape edges are pressed down firmly so no varnish can seep under it.

Many people buy varnish in quarts so you may have some left after your project. Make sure the lid is tapped down with a hammer and strain it the next time you use it. Some people store the cans upside down but that scares me. Varnish in smaller cans will expose less of it to the air as you work. In warm and humid weather, don't hesitate to thin it but always use the manufacturers recommended thinner. Start with as little as possible, add to it as necessary and stir it very gently. Unless you maintain a wet edge, overlapping brush marks will be obvious. A little thinner will make it easier to blend those brushstrokes together. Save plastic milk, orange juice, or booze bottles. Cut them off in the middle to make a container to tap the brush into. This will remove excess varnish from the brush and avoid bubbles or air contaminated varnish from getting back into the can.

Figure 9

A mayonnaise jar with a hole in the lid will hold a varnish brush using a small hole in the handle for a little piece of rod. Soaking in thinner, it won't harden for a few days.

Learning the "varnish stroke" is critical. The tip of the brush, with the right amount of varnish, should come down gently and in motion on the surface for the start of the varnish stroke. Then the flat of the brush comes down as a little more pressure is added. The pressure is gradually reduced until the brush tips come up off the surface at the end of the stroke. One secret of a perfect finish is bringing your head down close to the surface at the end of each stroke and looking toward the sun or the light to see if any imperfections require another stroke immediately. It may blind you but the varnish will look good.

After Forty Years --- Dave Wheeler

Badger brushes are perfect for the ultimate coat of varnish, but a good varnish job will need several coats. On a long job, you don't have to clean the brush each night. Fill a mayonnaise jar half full of the right thinner and punch a hole in the lid of the jar, just big enough for the handle. Push the handle of the brush up through the lid. Then put a piece of heavy wire or a large finishing nail through a small hole, drilled at the right height, to hold the bristles off the bottom but still completely covered with thinner. The next time you use the brush, get all the excess thinner out of it. Eventually, you will have to thoroughly clean the brush. Perfectionists use a new badger brush for the final coat.

In some seasons and places, good days are limited. A hard rain will pock the surface and you'll have to sand again but it's important to develop the right attitude. *Problems like that just give you an opportunity to put on another coat of varnish.* Protecting the wood is the prime reason to varnish it and additional coats are that much better. After a good weather forecast, start varnishing as early as possible. Dew may delay things but it's best to get done close to noon. Showers usually occur in the afternoon and I have seen a dark piece of teak get so hot from the sun, that the varnish crinkles before it dries.

Take a bucket to the work area with all the things you'll need, including a tack rag to pick up any dust, a can of the matching thinner and a rag to wash the wood thoroughly before you apply any varnish. Everything will be handy and the bucket may catch some drips.

Before you put anything else on the teak you may want to wash the wood with acetone first, to get the oils out. If you do, let it dry completely and then wash the wood again with a thinner compatible with the varnish or denatured alcohol. Find a piece of cloth that won't leave lint. The first coat of varnish should be thinned almost

50% to make sure it penetrates. There are also acrylic or epoxy based sealers. West System® epoxy can be used to seal out moisture and they will gladly send you information about using their products. The coats of West epoxy we put under our varnish not only sealed the wood but also helped create a beautiful surface. When we applied the West epoxy it was extremely hot, so we had to use a couple of tricks. A sweatband stopped sweat from dripping into the wet epoxy, which makes white spots that have to be removed. On a hot day the epoxy kicks off quicker than expected. The first mate helped me solve the problem by following me with the epoxy in an aluminum pie pan. I could keep brushing and the wide surface of the epoxy in the pie pan kept it from kicking off as quickly.

    West points out that it's important to use the sealing qualities of the epoxy to totally seal the wood under screw holes, behind moldings, or at the junction of wood and fiberglass surfaces. They recommend two or three coats of their 105 epoxy resin with 207 hardener. It should be allowed to cure before sanding. Then applying two or three coats of varnish will provide a longer lasting finish. Some people don't sand the first coat of varnish or the next, but it only takes a few minutes. I prefer to sand each coat with a sanding block covered with #320 wet or dry paper. The number of coats to apply is a matter of personal opinion, the time you have and your desire for perfection. Each coat puts another layer of varnish on top and sanding it with a block takes off the high spots which lets the low spots gradually fill in. It's best to let varnish dry for at least a day, perhaps two, before you sand it. If the varnish isn't hard enough it may roll up into little balls, which is difficult to fix. An absolute minimum of three coats will hold for a while, but six coats or more will give you a finish you can brag about.

FURNITURE STRIPPERS

Furniture stripping companies can be found in most cities. These companies have enormous vats, sometimes big enough to hold an entire dining room set. The furniture to be refinished is left in these vats full of solvent for a couple of days. The solvent removes every bit of paint or varnish and the refinisher has a fresh piece of wood to start with. It does have to be lightly sanded to remove the upstanding fibers and then sanded again after the first coat.

Look in the yellow pages for these companies under "Furniture Strippers." If you can't find anything under that heading, call some of the local antique dealers. This service can be a real help to boat owners. Think about those louvers you painstakingly sanded down, or the top of that door where the builders added some fancy carving. Varnished doors with multiple panels, or anything made of wood can be brought down to the natural finish, ready for you to make it look like new.

CHIP BRUSHES

I like those throwaway brushes. Sure, there are jobs that demand the best badger brush you can buy, but most of my projects fall in a somewhat lower category. It's expensive if you forget to clean a good brush right away and they do seem to get gummy eventually, no matter how hard you try to keep them clean. The cheapest brushes are the imported "chip" brushes. They actually work well except for all those blasted hairs that keep coming out.

I take each of my "chip" brushes and part the bristles down the center across the width of the brush. An old paring knife or a small putty knife will work fine. When the bristles are spread you may see that the hairs are not evenly spread. If this is the case, you have to take another "cut" at it. If they're spread apart evenly you should see the wooden stump of the handle down between the bristles. Holding the bristles apart, drip in a little cyanoacrylate or model airplane glue. A brand that is slightly liquid will spread out into the bristles before they dry. Some glues may soak into the wood too quickly and you'll have to add a touch more. This will not stop every bristle from coming out, but it improves my project and my patience about a thousand percent.

WATER-BASED PAINTS & VARNISHES

The Clean Air Act has produced a variety of laws covering everything from automobiles to chimney stacks, to paint and varnish. In the paint department, standards are written on the basis of volatile organic compounds, the fugitive solvents that disperse into the air. The amount is measured in pounds or grams. California, Alaska, Texas, New Jersey and New York have VOC regulations in place but it hasn't been smooth going. Technical problems have slowed things down. Some of the approved laws had to be put on hold for a while. Builders found that the best water-based marine varnish can approach the same gloss as the traditional varnishes and it requires half again as many coats to build to the same level. All the so-called water-based paints are emulsions. That is, they combine solvent and water.

Consumers have little faith in water-based paint. *It's supposed to repel water, not be mixed with it.* I understand. A couple of years ago I bought a quart of water-based bottom paint for my dinghy. Many other bottom paints had failed, so I was skeptical and concerned that it might wash away. It actually lasted longer than the previous bottom paints I had used and kept the dinghy bottom cleaner longer.

Low VOC paints have been in use on super-tankers, commercial and military vessels but most yacht builders are very reluctant to advertise "genuine water-based paint." That phrase is not likely to bring in new customers. Water-based interior varnish is more common but few manufacturers use water-based paints on the exterior. Water-based paints are just not found in marine stores.

The environmental people aren't going to give up until the VOC content is reduced. There are some good water based paints and varnishes out there that meet the Clean Air requirements and they can make life easier and safer. It might be worth your while to give them a try.

Chapter Five

MARINE INTERIORS

REFINISHING

Over the last decade, a substantial percentage of all new boats sold in the United States were built in the Orient. Teak is readily available in those countries and a many of these boats use teak veneer in their beautiful interiors. Most people think that since the veneer is inside and out of the weather, it will last forever with a little oil now and then. That isn't the case. As veneer gets old, the adhesive loses it's holding power. Tiny cracks develop that may not be apparent because they're so small. The veneer actually becomes porous and isn't strongly attached. That can result in serious problems that are difficult to repair.

Our first problem with teak veneer was the combination of dark teak and the tinted portholes down below. The light was so dim down there, we had to turn on the lights to find things during the day. A friend bought a new boat that had vinyl wallpaper in the interior. It looked quite handsome and my friend made the point that they didn't have to oil or varnish teak and if the wallpaper got dirty they could just wash it. There was a time when I would have scoffed at the idea of wallpaper on a boat. Things change. I decided to give it a try but it took a little research to find the right wallpaper. A strong pattern wouldn't work, stripes and grids would create matching and verticality problems, so we picked an "oatmeal" pattern. The new wallpaper made it lighter and brighter below deck and the remaining teak trim looked richer.

Figure 10

Light-colored, vinyl wallpaper below lightened up our stateroom and brought out the rich color of the teak doors.

We probably wouldn't have done anything more if it hadn't been for a big storm. One of the doors didn't get closed in time and rain soaked into the veneer in the pilothouse. The veneer not only came loose, but puckered up and split. Repairing veneer is nearly

After Forty Years --- Dave Wheeler

impossible because the veneer becomes a convex shape and you can't glue it back down. There may be experts who can deal with it but it's definitely beyond my capabilities.

We had professionals hang vinyl wallpaper on the walls below, which is the way to go if you have the slightest question about doing it yourself. Boats do have crazy corners and curved surfaces but if you've put up wallpaper back home you may be able to do the job yourself. On this new project, we found a professional paperhanger willing to work with us. He would do all the surfacing, filling in the depressions left where we pulled out loose veneer and then hang the vinyl wallpaper. We would varnish the solid teak, glue down some of the veneer that wasn't too loose to save and paint all the walls with sealer.

Deciding how much of the interior to cover is difficult. The interior surface of our pilothouse continues right down the companionway into the salon. There's no good place to stop, unless you add some small moldings as a break point and some areas may need moldings to finish off a corner. Like painting one room in a house, the refurbished area makes every other room look a little shabby.

Everything that could be unscrewed had to come off, including magazine racks, mug holders, fire extinguishers, speakers and pictures. A small file cabinet had to be emptied and unscrewed from the wall and louvered doors had to be refinished. The varnish had to be done first so it wouldn't get on the new wallpaper. We did the fronts of doors and drawers in satin finish teak.

Removing the damaged veneer was a major project. The veneer had come loose over a much larger area than we expected. In one spot a couple of layers of plywood had also delaminated under the veneer. One problem is determining how much of an area has come loose and whether it can be glued or has to be removed. If the veneer is loose, you may be able to pull it away until it resists where the glue is still holding. If the plywood underneath is delaminating, the loose material may be fairly thick and nobody wants to tear out an entire wall. A stiff piece of thin plastic or sheet metal can be cut about ten inches long and an inch and a half wide. (The first mate just bought a spatula with nearly the same dimensions.) With rounded corners on the probe or a spatula, you can poke about under the loose layers and find how far the delamination extends. That thin metal spatula is then used to insert a slow drying epoxy under the loose material. The loose laminate is fastened down with staples that are removed after the epoxy dries.

We had one ugly surprise. The vinyl wallpaper bubbled under the helm and when we peeled it off, we found that hydraulic fluid had leaked into the plywood. That fluid is oil, so it had to be washed with thinners and then blocked out with sealer. It's critical to seal all exposed wood with an oil base sealer. Failure to do this will cause more veneer to come loose. (My first mate also threatened death or deprivation if the carpet and upholstery were not completely protected once I started brushing on the white sealer.) Wallpaper paste is water based and if the wet paste soaks into the veneer, you may have to peel away the wallpaper again and rip out additional veneer bubbles. A good coat of oil base sealer forms a barrier. As the sealer is brushed on, additional cracks and crevices may show up that weren't evident before. All the depressions where veneer or plywood is removed have to be smoothed out with filler and a wide putty knife. Marine fillers are available, but polyester fillers can be used. It's easy to work with, cheaper, dries fast and waterproof.

The paperhanger arrived and set up a long folding table that fit in the salon right over our coffee table. For each area, the wallpaper was cut six to twelve inches larger in each dimension. The extra size is required to make sure there is enough material to be fit around elements like cabinet doors and curved corners on the inside of window frames. Our paperhanger used two large putty knives, six inches wide, one plastic and one metal. The plastic one was used to smooth down the wallpaper, driving out any air or bubbles of paste. The steel one was used to force the wallpaper into the edge of the window or door frame and hold it in place while the paper is cut to fit. Along a straight edge, it is simply a matter of holding the putty knife securely and cutting carefully. Around a curved corner, the paper has to be cut in from the corner so the paper will come down to the curve. It may be difficult to get the paper down in tight areas (like behind railings) but wallpaper paste dries slowly so you have time to work with it.

If you hire someone to hang the wallpaper, do plenty of research. Good sources include interior decorators and shops that sell wallpaper. You have to live with the results for a long time. We're certainly pleased with the results on our boat. Vinyl wallpaper may be one of the world's greatest marine inventions. No upkeep, except a little washing, is not a bad thing.

MARINE FABRICS

The price of our first powerboat was getting out of control and we had to cut back a bit. Among other things, I decided to make the V berth insert later so I asked for some of that fabric. It was several months before I made the insert and dug out the material. The new insert was so bright, when we took it down to the V berth, I thought the manufacturer had given us the wrong material. It was hard to believe the original material had faded that much. We're talking about fabric down in the V berth where the "sun don't shine." The only light comes in through the portholes and a hatch. A few years later we had a bigger boat and bought a sofa bed that became available when a big yacht was being redecorated. The household fabric on that sofa faded in four months.

Several years later I was working for the Ford Motor Company as an automotive designer. They have a policy of rotating people through different areas of the company and one day I found myself in charge of all interior materials and exterior colors. The fabric manufacturers and the experts in that department worked hard to give me an education and I learned many things I wish I had known earlier. Fabrics used in automobiles are expected to last for many years in heat, cold, humidity and, most important of all, in the sun's ultraviolet rays. Fabrics for use in automobiles retain colors much longer than household fabrics because they are solution dyed with higher pressures and stronger grades of chemicals and dyes. The construction of automotive material is selected for durability and velours have been popular fabrics. They're the same construction as velvet, which is woven as a double fabric and then sliced apart. As a result, the fibers in a velour stand on end and only the end of the individual fibers are directly exposed to sunlight or abrasion. Woven fabrics have horizontal fibers. The sides of those fibers and strands present more surface to the sun and are more easily damaged. Although you may not think of velvet or velour as a boat material, the automotive versions are extremely durable fabrics.

Figure 11
This helm chair is covered with a velour originally created for Lincoln automobiles. It has been in constant use for 15 years.

Automotive carpeting is much the same as commercial grade carpeting and will also last far longer, although it's much more expensive than household carpet. If you can work it into your budget when you buy a boat, it will eventually pay for itself by lasting longer and requiring less cleaning because of its stain resistance and durability. Many carpets claim to be stain resistant but this varies considerably. Our entire boat is carpeted. It seems a shame to cover all that beautiful teak parquet but it was a slippery surface when stepping inside on a rainy day. For some projects where the carpet will constantly be exposed to direct sunlight, there's a special type of carpeting you may want to look for. The shelf surface right under the back window of your car is always exposed to sunlight and special carpeting made of polypropylene fibers has been developed to stand up under the severe UV conditions in that area.

After Forty Years --- *Dave Wheeler*

It is standard policy that automobile companies keep some of their fabrics on hand for a period of time. Eventually they are sold to after-market sources. Automotive trim shops may be able to help you find materials that will work in your boat.

It isn't exactly a fabric, but we have some special covers on the windshield and on all the windows that get a lot of sun. They are made of a PVC coated polyester material that cuts down the amount of heat from the sun by well over seventy percent. We've found that it saves our varnish, cuts down the heat and keeps the sun from fading carpets or upholstery. It was originally made for outdoor furniture and its ability to reduce heat from the sun was discovered later. During the day, when the light is strongest outside, you can't see into the boat from the dock but we can see out just fine. Of course, we do have to remember not to run around in our skivvies at night because the situation is just the opposite when it's light inside and dark outside.

We also had snap-on screens, custom-made out of PVC material for the pilothouse doors. The outer edge of the screen snaps on to the inside of the door frame with soft foam, about 3/16th of an inch thick, between the screen and the door frame. The foam keeps out mosquitoes but must be closed cell foam or it will soak up water. On the inside edge of the screen snapped onto the door frames, a plastic zipper runs all the way from the bottom to inside the top edge. At the top, outside of the screen but inside the door frame, are two plastic strips that hold the screen when we roll it up out of the way. It requires no maintenance but once in a while we unsnap the whole thing, take it out on the dock and scrub off the salt grime.

Windshield covers are available in a variety of colors. We used white in the mistaken notion that white would reflect sunlight and help with heat reduction. We have since been told that the manufacturer's tests indicate that black blocks the most heat. I'm still not convinced, but whatever color you decide to use, these are great door screens. You can keep out bugs, cut down the heat and have a little privacy at the same time.

Industry fade tests made on solution-dyed acrylic fabrics showed they can last five times longer than residential fabrics. They also withstand the ravages of sun, saltwater and hard use. Many companies are offering new styling, brighter colors and patterns. An increasing number of cabin makeovers, from cushions to total interiors, including good looking fabrics for the interior, are available to make the first mate happy.

After Forty Years --- Dave Wheeler

Chapter Six

PLUMBING

THE HEAD

Nothing, not the wonders of electronic navigation or esoteric ports of call are topics of discussion as often as marine toilets, or heads. People ashore seldom talk about toilets, but conversations on boats frequently turn to, ah.... marine toilets. It's frustrating when such a basic piece of equipment betrays us, but regular maintenance can eliminate some of the problems. Various designs from vacuum operation to macerators, to holding tanks are debated but most agree that getting the material through the system is critical. Regardless how the stuff is propelled through the hoses, residues build up that eventually reduce the ability of the head to flush.

All heads are really pumps and to function properly they need clear inlet and outlet hoses. It doesn't matter whether you're in one of those rare areas where you can still discharge overboard, or if your outlet hose goes to a holding tank. The combination of salt water and the normal contributions constantly add to the wall thickness of the outlet hose. An old untreated outlet hose that had an original interior diameter of 1 ½ inches can be reduced to less than a half an inch, or shut off altogether. There are some ways to reduce the problem.

The best approach is to replace the hoses if you can. A boater near us in a marina in the Bahamas took his head hoses off and repeatedly slammed them down on the dock. It probably worked if it didn't damage the hoses but that's a desperate measure and the neighbors didn't think much of it. Another guy we know holds his breath and pours muriatic acid into the head as he constantly flushes it. He swears by it, but I have to admit I've always been a little afraid of that stuff, especially if you forget to hold your breath. In any case, it's not the right way to clean the head because the acid could eat away some vital parts in there.

We've found a solution, and that does seem to be the right word, for a concoction to pour in the head. It has kept the hoses clean and doesn't appear to have any ill effects that we can determine. Mix the following together:

1 gallon water
1-1/2 ounces of ammonia
1/2 cup of Pinesol™
1 cup of 20 Mule Team Borax Powder™

Pour one cup into each head, once a week, flush it half way through the system and let it sit for one to two hours.

PAPER TOWELS

There seems to be a breeze in every place available to put up a roll of paper towels and when the breezes blow, the paper towels come unrolled. Here is a way to eliminate the problem. Form a monkey's fist with 3/16th nylon line and leave about a foot of line. Put a screw eye in the rack behind the roll of paper. It should be level with the top of the roll. Tie the end of the line opposite from the monkey's fist on the screw eye. The remaining line should be long enough to allow the monkey's fist to hang below the center of the roll of towels. As the roll gets smaller, the monkey's fist will get lower, but the towels will stay put.

Figure 12
A small piece of line with a monkeys fist hanging over a roll of paper towels will keep it from unwinding.

WATER HEATERS

Our first water heater was marine grade, stainless and expensive. We were in the "nothing but the best" mode back when we first bought the boat and thought good stuff would last forever. Our water heater did last a long time but eventually it rusted and started leaking through the bottom. Replacing it turned out to be a problem. The best prices we could find for stainless marine water heaters were out of sight. We searched everywhere for a better deal. We even looked at small household water heaters although we weren't sure if they'd be good to use on a boat. The prices were definitely lower on the household models. None of them were stainless but then not all marine heaters were stainless and in the process, someone told us that stainless really means "stain-less." We also learned that the basic tanks, shells and most parts were identical between many household and marine water heaters. One advantage of the marine units is that the engines heat the water when you're running but we've never used the engines to heat water. At the dock we're plugged into the city electricity and at anchor, we have to run the generator enough to keep our batteries and the freezer happy. We bought one of the household units, went for a slightly larger capacity and still saved money. It's been in place for ten years and still working like a charm.

Chapter Seven

THE GALLEY

GALLEY TILE

Teak interiors are handsome, but food, cooking grease, or steam can ruin any wood used in the galley. Interior teak is usually veneer applied over plywood and the veneer can easily be damaged beyond repair. Simulated wood material like the Formica often used for counter tops seems to be a practical solution. However, the arrangement of our galley required the plastic material to be right next to genuine teak. The counter top material looked fine by itself but it sure looked plastic next to the real thing.

We settled on ceramic tile because it was handsome and it had a nice domestic look my wife liked. It turned out to be available at household prices instead of marine prices. Kitchen shops have a variety of colors and patterns that will look great in your galley, from sailing ships to our choice of a bronze/copper color that almost matches teak.

Buy extra tiles because they're not too expensive

and you'll need to practice cutting them. Cutting is done by scoring the surface and tapping the tile until it breaks. You can avoid much of the problem by stopping the tile short of a corner and finishing the edges with ceramic moldings that are also available from your local kitchen shop. Even if you get professional help, it's worth it in the long run. Ceramic tile is tough stuff. It doesn't show dirt; it's easy to clean and it will last *forever*.

Figure 13
Tile gave our galley a more domestic look and the tile will last forever.

LOUVERED GALLEY CABINETS

The overhead cabinets in our galley have louvers. As a matter of fact, practically every locker on the boat has louvers. I guess that's good for ventilation but the louvers on both sides of the galley cabinets bugged me. The cabinets are between the galley and the saloon, so one looks up at boxes of Frosted Flakes, pots, pans and miscellaneous cans looming through the louvers.

My wife helped me find some fabric that was heavy enough to hide the cereal boxes but still let a little air through. I used Monel staples to fasten the material inside the louvered doors and now nobody knows what's in there.

GALLEY TIPS

Nonskid will keep your plates in place and gasket cork under the things that stay on the galley counter will help hold them in place. If the weather is real bad or the container is unstable, the bottom of the shower is the best place. At least that's where my first mate puts our plants when the wind blows.

Nonstick pans are great aboard because they clean up easily. However, the coating can be scratched and damaged. If you stack them, pot holders or non-skid between each of the stacked pans will protect them.

Even though you use plastic bags inside your trash cans, once in a while you may have a leak or spill something. Waxing the inside of the trash cans will make cleanup easier.

Whoever came up with those official signs that MUST be posted, stating what cannot be dumped overboard, had no understanding of the power of first mates. She refused to have it in the galley, so we glued it inside the top of the trash can. That works for us.

Those fancy wood cutting boards are handsome but we always worried that the wood grain would be a haven for germs. A medical study group ran some tests and discovered that wood harbors fewer germs than most plastic cutting surfaces. It doesn't seem logical but that's the official word.

PRESERVING PLATES & KEEPING CUPS

Plastic cups won't break, they're cheap and there are a great variety of designs available in the marine catalogs, but I think coffee tastes better in a ceramic cup. After expressing those opinions, I couldn't very well argue when the first mate bought some beautiful earthenware dinnerware for the boat. The plates were no problem; we put circles of non skid material between them. The same product is used for shelving or put under carpets so they won't slide around.

We first hung cups by the handles but that didn't work. The cups rocked when the boat rolled and in heavy weather they were really swinging, so we had to come up with something else. We put two cup hooks in line across the cabinet, one in front and the other directly in back. A piece of nylon fish line was stretched across the cupboard, from front to back, in front of each row of cups. The line was positioned so the cups could not hang straight down but were held back at an angle by the line. The weight of the cups holds them in place against the fish line. The cabinets are athwartship, which makes the fish lines fore and aft but the weight of the cups also seems to be enough to keep the cups from moving sideways.

We had powerful quartering seas heading north from Spanish Wells last year -- one of those days when the bow moves in a big vertical circle -- and those cups didn't move at all.

Chapter Eight

AIR CONDITIONING

KEEPING COOL

If the air conditioning isn't cool as it should be, one of the first places to look is at the water being discharged outside. Sediment that comes in with the salt water will eventually gather in the low spots of the hoses and reduce water flow. Checking the water outlets regularly and cleaning out the hoses has kept us cool. We made a little gadget that plugs a dockside water hose directly into the incoming hose and then into the outgoing hose. We let it run for fifteen minutes or so.

The water coming in through the incoming hose also cleans the coils of the air conditioner. In most boats the condensation from the A/C goes first into a pan under the unit and then into the bilge. If the drains from the pans stop up, the excess water can appear anyplace below the unit and you may have wet carpet or water in a place that's hard to clean up. We once lost a shelf of books. The solution is to put a little Clorox in the drain pans now and then. That will keep the drain hoses open and stop the overflows.

Up north, in an effort to maximize heat, air deflectors on the outlets are common. We found they can be used with air conditioning in our boat to direct the cool air where it will do most good.

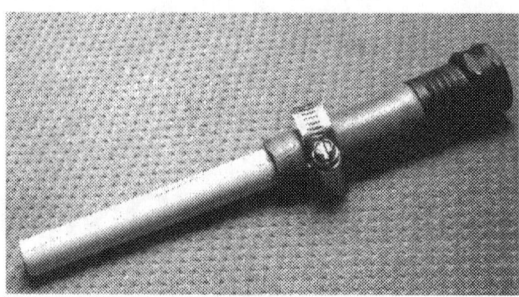

Figure 14

Attach this to a water hose. Insert it in the water hose for the air conditioning unit. Let it run for 15 minutes. This will remove debris from the raw water side of the system which will improve performance.

INSULATION

Every home up north has insulation and weather stripping to keep cold air out. Boats can also benefit from being insulated. In the fall, in the north, it can extend the cruising season and in the south, it can be a lifesaver in the hot and humid summers. A well-insulated boat will keep cold air in and hot air out when you run the air conditioning. We worked on our boat during the winter months in the north and accomplished a lot because we were comfortable inside and had that extra time. Sealing and insulating your boat will make a major difference in the temperature inside and it will save money regardless of your latitude. Insulation can be improved in virtually every boat. Most boats do have insulation between the living quarters and the engine room. It not only improves the temperature difference, it reduces the noise from the engines or a generator.

In most cases the hull of the boat is built first and then the interior is created with wood panels. In some contemporary boats, shells that create interior compartments are dropped into the hull. Entire heads, including the showers, sinks and facilities are often used. V-berth areas including the berths can be installed and even complete galleys can be lowered in place. In every case there is open space between those units and the hull. If there's enough space and it can be reached, it might be used for storage. This is often the case because the exterior hull is curved or convex and the inside sections are usually rectangular. If you've slept up in the bow at anchor and the inside of the hull is right next to you, the noise of the waves hitting the hull gives you a clue of how little there is between you and the water out there.

If you can be present when the boat is being built, you can decide which of these voids should be saved for storage and which might be better used for insulation. We've seen storage areas that are too narrow to be very useful. Basically, the idea is to create a cocoon that will separate hot air from cool air, or noisy areas from quiet ones. In addition to temperature and noise control, there are also benefits in eliminating situations where condensation can form inside the hull and eventually create problems with rust, rot or corrosion.

There are many ways and places to insert fiberglass batting, Styrofoam, or other insulation but the ideal solution is having it built into the boat. If you do it yourself, there's a new insulation material called Miraflex from Owens Corning. It is the first real change since that itchy, irritating fiberglass insulation was developed. This stuff feels like soft cotton. You can crawl into a warm engine room with batts of it and not have to head for the shower instantly to stop the irritation.

It's more evident up north, but even the doors on some very expensive boats let a draft come in around the edges. As part of a survey, hose the boat with a vengeance before you take delivery. You may be surprised at the amount of water that gets inside and this is the best time to eliminate leaks. Later on, when the interior and the furnishings are in place, those leaks may be difficult to find or create more problems.

There is variety of weather stripping for doors and windows, from compressed foams to mechanical closures. The most common solution is compressed foam material between the door and the frame. Another is a sealing strip that closes by forcing a thin piece of rubber to rub across the bottom of the door frame. In the south, these have the added virtue of keeping the creepy-crawlies out. The local hardware store may have what you need, but if you buy weather stripping made of a foam material, make sure it is closed cell and does not hold water. If the weather stripping has metal parts, make sure any exposed metal won't rust. Once you look at the big openings around your doors and windows, you'll wonder why this project never occurred to you before.

VENTILATION

There are circumstances where you don't need or want air conditioning. Sometimes a good fan will be enough to keep you comfortable and at anchor there is no A/C unless you run the generator.

Hatches bring air, light and sometimes rain into the boat. There seems to be a difference of opinion about the proper positioning of hatches. Most marine architects have them hinged at the front and opening from aft, so that a great wave won't come over the bow and sink your boat. That makes sense, but on our trawler we turned the foredeck hatch around so the breezes at anchor come directly into the boat. Wind scoops, available in most marine catalogs, were designed for sailboats. I don't have anything up above to tie them to so we had to experiment.

One simple approach was making two side pieces that fit in the sides of the opened hatch. We found that camping catalogs offer a hatch cover with louvers that are basically open all the time and aren't supposed to leak in the rain. These are made of translucent plastic but they still cut down the light. One interesting approach we saw on a sailboat, was positioning the dinghy on the foredeck, bow forward and raised to become an air scoop.

Our final solution was an air scoop made of strong fabric to withstand heavy winds and designed for our boat. Any good canvas person could help design one for you. Ours hooks across the back of the hatch and is snapped to the top of the bowstaff and under the rails on either side of the foredeck. The bowstaff gives it a high center and the attachment to the rails creates a wide mouth that really gathers air. The overall height enables us to open or shut the hatch without removing the air scoop. Since the scoop covers a lot of area over the hatch, we can leave the hatch open in a light rain. It's been a blessing at anchor when we sleep up in the V berths The air flows right in and keeps us cool even in the middle of summer.

After Forty Years --- Dave Wheeler

Chapter Nine

TELEPHONES

LAND LINES

If you plan to stay or be based in one marina, you will probably want a telephone. This is also important if you want to use a computer. However, be prepared for some problems. The trouble started when we decided to move to another slip after two years in the same marina. The ding-a-ling that ran the switchboard told everyone we were *gone*. I had to go see her to prove I still existed, which is when we put in a private line. It took a little negotiating with the marina and the telephone company but we worked it out. Since we were making some telephone changes, we decided to put in another instrument and an answering machine. The man from the telephone company was knowledgeable and helpful, so I asked him to come aboard and help us install lines for the new instrument and the answering machine. He surprised me with a vehement, "No." The man absolutely refused to step aboard the boat. He said that company policy would not allow him to touch anything on any vessel.

After Forty Years --- Dave Wheeler

The company will add internal lines in a land based residence for an additional service fee, but NO BOATS.

The FCC changed the rules in 1977 and today anyone can buy and install their own telephone equipment, even on a boat. The rules say that you should notify the local telephone company when you install a new instrument and provide them with the FCC and serial number information listed on the bottom or the back of the phone. I don't believe many people do that.

Our local hardware store carries telephone wires and parts. The local manager was helpful and had some good suggestions. He told me that although voltages on a telephone are very small, it takes more power to make the phone ring. The ringing voltage can give you a shock and could affect a pacemaker. If you're adding a new telephone, take the handset off the hook on one of the other phones. This keeps the phone from ringing and eliminates shocks from the ringing voltage. Our friendly hardware man told me a couple of other things that seemed to be obvious. Don't fiddle with telephone lines during a thunderstorm and don't cut into an electrical wire, mistaking it for a phone line.

The telephone company will be happy to sign you up for a private line but there are considerations. Every marina is different. Some have telephone wire and outlets built right into the docks, others have little or no accommodation for a private line. In that case, you'll have to pay the telephone company to bring the connection and a plug to your slip. In a few marinas they won't let you put in a line unless you've contracted to stay at that marina for a year. In any case, depending on what is required, the telephone company is going to charge you to run the wires to your boat.

The connection from the dock to the boat is a 50 foot yellow cable, built with standard telephone plugs at each end. However it's possible to buy heavy black cable normally used for construction, exterior situations or being buried below ground. This type of cable is sold in lengths far bigger than you need, but it's much cheaper than the yellow cable and you can make a cable that will reach *anywhere*. Male and female ends are available in most catalogs.

Local marine stores and marine catalogs have plastic or stainless steel telephone inlets for boats. These have weatherproof, spring-loaded snap lids and often a cable TV connector as well. The inlets are square but require a 2 1/2" circular hole. Set the inlet in the opening to mark where the four mounting screws will go and drill 1/8" mounting holes. Estimate the length of telephone wire you'll need inside and fasten the ends of the wire to the inlet before you screw it to the hull. The rubber sealing gasket should be over the wire between the hull and the inlet. The four screws go right through the inlet and the gasket. The inlet has letters to indicate where each wire should go. Be sure to read the instructions carefully, in this case, *the letters do not indicate color.* The back of the marine inlet is marked with "R" (for ring) where the red wire goes, "T" (for tip) where the green wire is attached and "GR" (for ground) where the yellow wire is fastened. It isn't necessary to use the black wire.

There are two basic types of telephone wires. One is the flat wire with the standard plastic plugs that go into modular jacks on almost any telephone device. The other one is a round wire (called an extension cable) that is used for longer distances. This is the type of wire you will be attaching to the inlet. The end of the extension cable inside the boat is wired to a modular block that accepts the standard interior plastic plugs, which are called "4-pin modular connectors".

The four wires in the cable from the inlet are attached first to a terminal block just inside the hull.

Make sure to check the instructions every time. *These blocks have four letters that do indicate wire colors.* If one of the instruments to be installed is close and another is a long way from the terminal block, you can put more than one set of wires on each of the screws. One set from the back of the inlet, (the incoming line), one for the long run and one for a nearby modular connector. For example, three yellow wires could go to the attachment screw with the letter "Y," and three of each color to the appropriately marked screws.

A second option is to go directly to a modular jack inside and change over to the flat interior telephone wire with the plastic plugs. These wires are available in many different lengths and there are connectors of all kinds, whether you want to split the wire into two cords, three cords, or add to the length of a cord you have. It's possible to do the entire boat with the standard interior telephone wires although it may add up to a lot of wires and connectors. The plastic plugs also require a larger hole if the wire goes through a bulkhead. Four wire extension cable can provide the neatest job with modular jacks at each point where you want to put an instrument, or at strategically located points where you may wish to have an instrument in the future.

A plan or a sketch before doing any wiring will result in a neater job. How many phones will there be and where should they be located? How will the wires get to each of those places? Fax machines, computer modems or answering machines require special consideration. A surge protector for your phone line will keep power spikes from damaging modems, faxes or answering machines. After the predetermined number of rings, an answering machine may take control of the incoming line. ADSL or broadband has changed many of those things. Since computer frequencies and telephone frequencies are different, you can be working on the computer and answer the phone when it rings. Another little difference is that surge protectors will mess up ADSL lines. Unless you read all the instructions on any of these devices, you can get in trouble and going back to change the wiring is an ugly job. I know, I've done it.

SEAGOING CELLULAR

Cellular phones are everywhere. People drive, walk and probably do a lot of other things with a tiny phone pressed to their ear. Many are addicted to them and can't go anywhere without their phone. Meanwhile, more features are being added and the phones are getting so small somebody may swallow one.

The United States is not the leader in cellular phone development. European countries have been ahead of us for at least ten years. Finland has the best phones and last year Nokia global sales were worth nine and a half billion dollars. Almost 60% of the Finns have a mobile phone. Japan will deploy their high-speed national network in March of 2001, and is introducing mobile videophones. As Europe and Japan compete, the US is struggling to keep up. The Europeans are at least 3 years ahead of us because they have a single digital network--Global System for Mobile Communications. Our manufacturers keep fighting over whose system is used, losing research and product development time.

To be fair, part of the reason for Europe's lead in mobile telephones is the fact that their basic telephone systems were so bad. If you've ever used a phone in Paris or Spain, the struggle between language and the outrageous and expensive telephone system just about drives you crazy. As a result, the people in Europe were desperate for a new system and they took to the mobile telephone like thirsty sailors.

After Forty Years --- Dave Wheeler

The Coast Guard says they're getting an increasing number of cellular calls and they don't like it. They have systems in place to locate the source of a VHF call but can't locate a cellular phone. They also say that many connections are dropped when people realize the cost is mounting, which often happens before the Coast Guard gets all the needed information. The USCG needs all that information to protect their budgets. Every call is recorded and the station winds up with a statement of how many dollars worth of marine vessels they saved. I was in the auxiliary when a 727 aircraft declared an emergency over Lake Erie. It didn't crash but a 42 ft. Coast Guard vessel was dispatched and, shortly thereafter, records showed a Coast Guard vessel saving a multi-million dollar aircraft and 89 passengers. This type of information is used when congress plans budgets.

Nevertheless, the cellular people will win. Marinas are receiving an increasing number of cellular calls from approaching boats. The phones will improve and offer more features and there are too many of them out there to ignore, but most important of all, people like cellular phones.

Chapter Ten

PESTS

BUGS

Sooner or later every boat gets bugs. It is simply not possibly to visit scores of marinas, especially in the south and the tropics, without having bugs come to visit. Jimmy Buffett says "changes in latitude bring changes in attitude." The man knows what he's talking about — only I don't think he had bugs in mind. We moved south after I retired and down here people are proud to have the bug man's truck in their driveway. It shows they're clean people and can afford to have the bug man visit. Up north, my grandma would have called the police if somebody parked a bug truck in our driveway. We might have had a bug or two but up there *nobody* talked about that outside the house.

We came down the ICW, pure as the driven snow and suddenly, bugs showed up. Not one, mind you, but bunches of them kept appearing out of nowhere. We sprayed, we put boric acid in all the corners but sooner or later there was another one. Frankly, it's a little scary to turn on the lights and have one go running across the floor. Before you can react it's gone, back into some place where you can't get it.

It was a typical hot and humid day when we pulled into a famous marina in the Carolinas. I was soaking wet after we got the boat secured and went below to wash up. As I dried my hands, the biggest roach I have ever seen came in through the open porthole. I grabbed it with a paper towel and went out to dispose of the body. The marina had just been taken over by new owners and as I arrived in the cockpit, the new manager arrived with flowers for the first mate and a flowery welcoming speech as well. It just didn't seem polite to interrupt his speech while I threw the bug over, so I stood there and held it while I smiled and nodded. The bug wasn't dead. It wiggled and struggled while I listened to the marvels of the new marina. It kept squirming and I kept squeezing to keep it from getting away.

Since that time a number of companies have come out with little discs that attract and kill roaches. I really hate to put this in print, or even say it, but we haven't seen a roach on our boat for several years. We keep a list of "Combat Zones" so we know where we put the last ones and when we should put out new ones.

We were anchored in the Little Shark River on Florida's west coast and, although people had warned us about the mosquitoes there, we hadn't seen any. Our peace was suddenly interrupted when an extremely ugly hornet flew into the boat. It had a yellow green head and strange stripes. I was wondering if it was poisonous when my wife arrived with the swatter. She kept missing it and when she did connect, it kept right on flying around. By that time it was one angry hornet. I decided to get the vacuum but the deadly hornet flew out the door.

We were on a peaceful mooring in Royal Harbour in the Bahamas one evening when a "Money Bat" flew in the open door. These are large moths with a wingspan of at least three inches and one flying into the boat tends to scare you. After I recovered I decided to catch it and turn it loose outside. I grabbed it with a paper towel and headed toward the door while it struggled. Ordinarily moths don't struggle, but this one twisted its body like an angry cat in my grip. I was so impressed I asked one of the locals in Spanish Wells about the moths. He said they weren't uncommon and there was a superstition that if one came in your house, you were going to receive some money. I kept waiting but there weren't any checks in the mail, but then there wasn't any mail in Royal Harbour either.

BLIND MOSQUITOES

Figure 15

Blind mosquitoes are a real problem in fresh water areas of the south. The photo shows sparse coverage compared to the two- inch deep layer we found on the decks.

After Forty Years --- Dave Wheeler

We cruised up the St. Johns River with friends on a boat named "Betty Ann" and one night we anchored in Salt Cove, at the northeast corner of Lake George. It was a lonely spot and we could hear some strange sounds in the distance, but I convinced my wife that it was just tree peepers looking for mates. We did agree with the other boat to keep the VHF on, more because of solace than security. We got a call from "Betty Ann" *at dawn* the next morning and I'm not sure I answered cordially. Betty was breathless -- "Don't go outside! There are thousands of bugs two inches deep on the deck and I slipped and fell." Holy Creepy-Crawlies! The bugs *were* two inches deep out there! Something had to be done, so I dug out some hose and a water pump and started washing them off with water from the lake. The things just flew over to the other side of the boat. We hosed off as many as we could and then headed to Palatka.

It was a long ride but there were no more problems. As soon as our boat was tied up, we started hosing off bugs. The things would still fly to the other side of the boat, leaving a residue of green slime that wouldn't wash away. Some went to the boats across the dock. We apologized but they said, "Don't worry about it. Boats come in here all the time with blind mosquitoes." We had never heard of blind mosquitoes. Many people call them "midges." These little mosquitoes are most unusual, they don't bite at all – otherwise, two boats might have been found in Lake George, with hollow bloodless bodies aboard. Much later, we found that among the millions of bugs on the boat, thousands had hidden away and died in places we opened months later.

The conservation people have struggled for a long time to find a solution. Today there are fewer mosquitoes but the birds, turtles and alligators still make it a wildlife photographer's paradise. The river and its wildlife are beautiful. It was a haven from hurricanes and a unique cruise, but the next time we may not go between April and November.

After Forty Years --- Dave Wheeler

After Forty Years --- Dave Wheeler

Chapter Eleven

LITTLE THINGS

FIDDLES & CAPS

Fiddles are the proper name for the moldings marine designers put around the edges of tables and cabinets. They were originally designed to keep your grog from sliding off the table in a rough sea. Fiddles may look very traditional, but they stick up above the table surface about an inch and there's no way in the world you can get a chart flat enough to plot a course.

A friend of mine is an expert with a table saw and with his help, we made a teak cap that fits over the top of the fiddled table. If you do nothing else with it, this project creates a good-looking piece of furniture. Our table is in the pilothouse and we eat breakfast up there every morning so we can see out over the bay and watch what's happening in the marina.

After Forty Years --- Dave Wheeler

Figure 16
The new plotting table

The first time I started to plot some courses, I realized that dividers and compasses were going to punch holes in that beautiful teak surface, so we added an 1/8 inch piece of Lexan to protect the top. Later I changed to Plexiglas. It does scratch more easily but we turn it over when it gets too messy and the marks don't show as much. When I'm going to do some serious cutting, I put down a self-healing plastic mat, available in most stores selling drafting supplies or sewing materials. It covers up the handsome teak but we put a chart of the West Indies under the plastic to track where friends are traveling or which way a storm is moving. At my end, I keep three pages of "Month-at a Glance" calendars to record when we're supposed to go places or do things like checking the batteries. All this does cover the top but you can still see a little magnificent joinery work on the corners.

The top of the cap is 1/2 inch teak, veneered plywood. The edges are solid teak, 1/2 inch thick and 2-1/4 inches high. The height depends on how high the moldings are. The cap should completely cover the top and edges of the table. Three quarter inch teak can be used but it will add to the weight. Teak is available from some local yards and several mail order companies specializing in hardwoods. I now have a flat surface for my charts and a great storage area under the cap for brochures, pads, triangles and even a few skinny books.

THE BRASS LAMP TRICK

My wife had some solid brass lamps that had been handed down in her family for several generations, which she thought would look nice on the boat. I imagined those heavy lamps flying around in rough seas but she was determined to keep them. A kindly old lamp maker showed me how to solve the problem. Most lamps are made the same way; the light socket is screwed into the end of a metal rod, which goes down through the body of the lamp. The bottom section of the lamp is usually concave and has a small hole the size of the rod. The rod is threaded at the bottom and a washer and locknut in the concave area hold the lamp together.

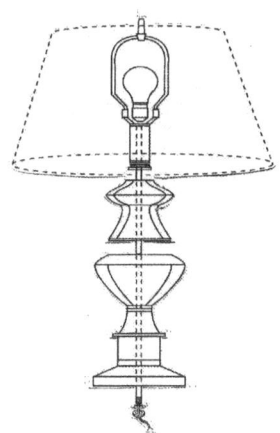

Figure 17
A lamp fastened to the table by lengthening the center post to bolt it in place.

I took our lamps apart and replaced the rods with

others also threaded at the bottom but about three inches longer. These rods were long enough to go through holes in the top of the cabinets where we wanted the lamps. The electrical cord usually comes down through the rod and is brought out through the side of the base. In our setup, we simply let the cords come all the way down through the rods to the inside of the cabinets. Fender washers and locknuts screwed tightly against the inside of the cabinets make those lamps steady as a rock in any kind of weather. Just one caution--*be absolutely sure where you want the lamps before you drill the holes!*

PORTHOLE COVERS

Portholes are sometimes at a level that makes it easy to see in, particularly at night when the lights are on. A friend frosted his ports by putting varnish on the glass with a sponge but that's a very permanent move. I cut out some pieces of a cheap textured plastic from the local hardware store the size and shape of the port and put them in place with Velcro. We could take them down during the day and put them up as needed. I was a little pleased with myself until my wife came up with a better approach. (She does that a lot.) My solution had two problems. The cheap plastic cracked easily and if they weren't on the ports, they were in the way.

The first mate made covers of fabric and bound the edges to make them durable. Fabric provides the option of many colors and patterns. It can also be held in place with Velcro and that allows you to just undo the top and let it hang in place out of the way. If you're even neater you can fold them up and put them away. A light fabric or frosted vinyl will let in the most light.

DOCKSIDE FILTERS

Our boat has a water filter in the engine room built into the water system. As we traveled to different marinas, I kept seeing boats with water filters out on the dock and I thought it was too bad that they didn't have a proper inboard filter like mine. Some of those big boats could obviously afford to have a built in water filter but one even had two filters in line on the dock. I finally asked someone why they had the water filters out on the dock and they explained that outside filters catch the bad stuff before it gets into the boat. Deposits form on the inside of the water lines over time and it's a lot easier and cheaper to change a hose than replacing a copper line inside the boat. I'm still learning.

SCREWED UP HOSES

A friend who went on a cruise with us pitched right in and took care of some of the chores. A few days later I got out a hose and it was not only tied, but the ends were screwed together. My guest explained that screwing the ends together keeps water from running out and keeps bugs and miscellaneous stuff from getting in it.

CUTTING MATS

Cutting mats are standard in many design, architectural or drafting offices. They have layers of different plastic, with a harder material at the bottom and a softer self-sealing plastic on the surface. Professionals use mats with a variety of grids in centimeters or inches, some with type size lines or other patterns. The one I had on the boat was several years old and getting tired, so I priced a new one and found they cost more than I thought. I kept the old ratty one, but if something needed cut, I risked putting gashes in the teak tabletop

My wife told me about some mats she had seen in a fabric and craft store and I found a solution to protecting my tabletop. They have gray plastic cutting mats designed for sewing purposes, like cutting out fabric patterns or quilting. They're self sealing, with orange gridlines in inches. I found three sizes that could be used for my purposes: 12x28, 18x24 and 24x36.

NEEDLENOSE FIDS

A pair of needlenose pliers can be made into an excellent fid for making splices or any other marlinspike work. Right out of the package, the shape of the pliers jaws and the regular handles are ideal for a fid. Round off the noses with a file and then polish them smooth. The pliers have several advantages. With the jaws together, you can use them as a regular fid and since they're wider on one side, you can spread strands by twisting them sideways. If you need even more room between strands, force the pliers open and spread the strands apart. Use them as pliers to pull a stubborn strand through a narrow spot, or to tighten up a splice. To undo a stiff knot that's been tied for some time, work the pliers in to get a good grip and then twist the pliers, pulling one of the lines in the knot loose.

TONGUE DEPRESSOR TOOLS

Tongue depressors are commonly used to stir paint with, but they can be used in many other ways. They make good wedges to level things or to make room for air to get under something. You can break off pieces to make surface protectors for C clamps and that's only the beginning.

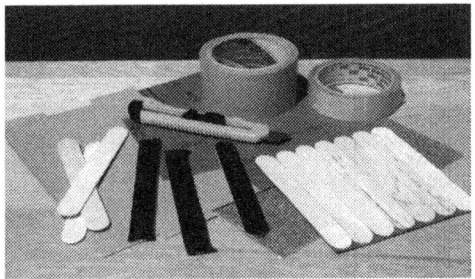

Figure 18
Tongue depressors can be used for many things, from mixing epoxy to protecting a surface from a vice.

Glue a piece of outdoor carpet to a tongue depressor and you will have an excellent tool for cleaning louvers. Depressors can be glued on the back of the carpet with fast drying glue and then cut out. Depending on the space between the louvers, carpet can be applied to one side or both.

Tongue depressors make a great tool for two part epoxies. They can be easily cut in half with sharp scissors. Use one half for part 1 and the other half for part 2 and the two epoxy components will never get mixed together. The square ends make good scoops and you can easily compare the amount on the first half with the amount on the second half. Use another half depressor cut square at the end to mix the epoxy together and the square end can be used almost like a putty knife.

My favorite tongue depressor tool is a homemade "emery board." They can be made with any number of sandpaper grades, from 50 to 600 and they're very handy for sanding in tight places. Two way tape is available in most art & craft stores. You can make one sanding tool at a time with one inch wide two way tape, or go whole hog and cover the entire back of a sheet of sandpaper with the two way tape. Lay down the depressors, side by side, on the sandpaper and cut them all out at once. Make sure to use a knife with replaceable blades because cutting the sandpaper will completely destroy a knife blade. Almost all tongue depressors are warped lengthwise and so they should be laid down with the hollow side up to get good adhesion to the surface. Trim the sandpaper to match the round end of the depressors if you wish, but they work just as well with the square corners left in place.

VINYL LETTERING AND DESIGNS

If you've had some drafting, drawing or artwork experience, you can make your own lettering or design you'd like to have on your boat. If the letters are the name of the boat or registration numbers, be sure to check the Coast Guard regulations for size and contrast. You can easily meet their requirements and still have the color you want, with better looking numbers than the ready made ones. The color of the lettering or design has to contrast with the color of your hull, therefore, if it's a white flag, you have to put it on a dark background or add an outline around it. Proper spacing is important for lettering. For example, you need more space between an "M" and an "I" than between an "A" that follows an "F." Many sign companies can make lettering in several typefaces on a computer designed for the purpose of cutting out the letters. On lettering projects, you might be well advised to go to a local sign company. Pick out a typeface they have in stock and let them make the letters.

The area where the letters will be placed should be clean and buffed if necessary, but *not waxed*. At any point, you can change your mind and take the letters off. If there's old vinyl lettering that you want to remove, heat the letters with a hair dryer or cautiously with a heat gun. Get a corner loose with a fingernail (be careful, it's hot), or with a carefully used putty knife and the letters should peel right off. If a residue of any kind is left, it can be removed with a citrus solvent called Goo Gone.

My wife and I are Hams. We both have amateur radio licenses and we're members of the Waterway Net. The Net relays messages and weather reports you can hear offshore or in the Bahamas with a high frequency radio. We thought it would be nice to have our call signs on the boat, so I got busy on our computer and tried different fonts and sizes until I found something we liked. I printed them as large as I could and then had them enlarged to several different sizes on a copy machine. I taped the copies on the side of the boat to see if they were the right size and if they looked the way we wanted. The largest copies were pretty ragged looking and after we selected a size and typeface we liked, I cleaned up the letters as I traced them.

The material used for the letters is a thin vinyl sheet with a powerful adhesive on the back. It's sold in rolls, on a heavy backing paper. 3M™ made the first of this material that I had experience with. It was used in the automotive industry back when there were cars with all sorts of graphics and stripes. Look in the yellow pages under "sign supplies". These places have the material in a variety of colors. We also found local sign companies are usually very helpful.

After I corrected and traced the letters on paper, I used a silver Prismacolor pencil number 949 on the back to make a "carbon copy." In our case, the vinyl material was dark and silver shows well on it. If it had been a light color, I might have used a Stabilo soft lead pencil number 8008. Both types of pencil will rub off, so I kept a piece

Figure 19
Vinyl lettering or designs for your boat are not too difficult to apply.

of typing paper under my hand as I did the cutting. I taped the vinyl down and also taped the tracing paper so it would stay exactly in place. When I thought I had it all traced, I left one edge taped in place and lifted the other edge to look. If you missed a line it's easy to correct because the tracing is still exactly in place.

Cut out the letters gently with an Exacto knife, so that you cut through the vinyl but not through the backing paper. Backing paper holds the letters in place until you're ready to transfer them to the boat. Cutting will be easier if you have the material taped to a slightly larger piece of cardboard or plastic, so you can rotate it to get the best angle to cut each line. As you cut out the letters, remove the background material so the letters or designs are the only things on the backing. Be sure you've cut all around each letter or the vinyl will tear when you try to take off the background. Leave a piece of the vinyl under the tape at the corners so you don't

After Forty Years --- Dave Wheeler

pull the tape off as you remove the background material. Tape won't hold on the waxy surface of the backing paper alone.

After cutting and only the design or letters are on the backing, you'll need a piece of the application material, which is a translucent paper with an adhesive on it that's less powerful than the adhesive on the vinyl. Cut a piece close to the same overall size of the design and press it, adhesive side down, over the letters. You might want to use a plastic squeegee to press the paper down tightly. Before you do anything else, make some registration marks on the application material and on the boat, so you can place the lettering exactly where you want it.

Now peel the backing off, leaving the letters held to the paper with its weak adhesive. Spray the area where you plan to put the letters with slightly soapy water. The water will allow you to slide the letters around to the correct position before the adhesive grabs the surface. On the reverse side ,the letters have the strongest adhesive so when you apply it to the surface and squeegee out the water, the design or letters will stick while the paper peels off. Check the letters for bubbles and try to squeegee the air or water, out to the side. Use a plastic putty knife, after smoothing the end of the blade with 600 sandpaper. Treat it gently for a day or so until the adhesive has maximum strength.

STORAGE

There is no way a marine architect can put together all the building blocks of a boat, like companionways, heads, berths, or galleys without leaving a few empty spaces. All the spaces people normally use are square places and they just don't fit together in the curved shape of a hull. As a result, there's a surprising amount of unused space on every boat, it just isn't apparent. Once you start thinking about what's behind that bulkhead or under that cabinet you'll find all kinds of little storage spots and a few empty spaces that are unexpectedly large.

There are a few obvious, unused spaces on every boat. Those are the ones big enough to put in shelves or build an interior compartment. Marine catalogs offer hinged teak doors, complete with frames and all you have to do is cut the right size hole and fasten the frame in place. Many other spaces are just waiting to be found.

Sometimes there's a small space above top drawers where you can add a small hidden tray to store documents and papers. There's usually plenty of room below the bottom drawers because the hull angles down below the drawer compartment. Steps or companionways often conceal room below. These are sometimes neglected by the builder because they're awkward places to build storage and expensive to include. Most lockers or cabinets have unused room at the top and many hanging lockers have room at the top for a small shelf. A storage locker in one boat had almost as much room in the top, up above the door, as the area we normally used. We also have a long seat in the pilothouse with a back that's really a wooden box with a cushion on the front. We cut a hole at the end to fit a standard louvered insert, fastened it with two screws, and we had a place to store charts, skeet guns, rolls of tracing paper and a few moldings.

SUPER HONKERS

Bridges can be a problem. I call on channel 13, then on 16 before I start to worry. Maybe I used the wrong bridge name, as bridge names on charts can be different than the name the bridge answers to. Finally, I blow the horn to get their attention, which doesn't always work. Therefore, I decided I wanted a BIG horn -- a really big horn!

We found a 37 inch air horn made for large trucks. I learned that UCLA used the same horns at football games but powered them with a twenty pound CO_2 bottle, about two feet high and eight inches in diameter. It isn't easy to get one of those tanks because the gas companies want to rent the tanks and sell you the gas. I finally found a tank and put a standard gas regulator on it. I started with just a couple of pounds of pressure and then gradually increased it until it had the power I wanted.

Trucks have lanyards in their cabs to blow the horn, so we made one for our console with a little touch of marlinspike.

The people at UCLA told me their horns last for half the football season. We're not honking to celebrate every touchdown so ours will last longer. At first we used CO_2 but I had a machinist make a custom valve so the tank can be filled at any dive shop. Most states require that you have the tanks tested at regular intervals. The drawback is that the tank takes room and it's heavy to get out for a refill. I don't really care. That horn really knocks bridge tenders off their chairs.

STEREO SPEAKERS

Stereo speakers in marine catalogs are good looking and well designed, but they don't look like they belong on a boat. The interior of our boat is mostly teak so we were looking for small speakers that would blend in with the teak. There was enough space between the interior teak surface and the hull to install some small speakers but the speakers we wanted didn't seem to exist. Thinking about it that night at dinner, I found the solution right in front of me. The trivets on our table were basically a teak grating with a rectangular pattern of openings about half an inch square.

We bought a small black speaker that would fit between the wall and the hull, recessed the speaker and then fastened the trivet, which was now a speaker grill, over it. The black stereo speaker was hardly visible. If the speaker is not black, staple a piece of dark speaker cloth on the inside of the trivet. Most speaker cloths are made of plastic materials and are relatively waterproof. These installations look like they came with the boat, but I would offer one caution— don't install speakers anywhere near your compass. The better the speaker, the bigger the magnet it has. Magnets can affect a compass and make it point in directions you don't want to go.

SCUPPER STAINS

Water coming out of the scuppers or from bilge pump outlets often leaves an ugly brown stain on the hull where the water runs down. The trick is to get the stream of water out away from the hull. With a little searching, you should be able to find a piece of flexible tubing that will just fit the round outlets from a through hull and divert the water away from the hull.

The oblong scuppers along decks are harder to deal with. The easiest solution is a piece cut from a white Clorox bottle rolled at the edges to fit in the opening. It tends to open after you insert it, and combined with a little silicone, the piece will seal itself as it presses against the inside of the scupper. It does protrude from the hull but it's somewhat flexible and, even if knocked loose, it's easy to glue back in.

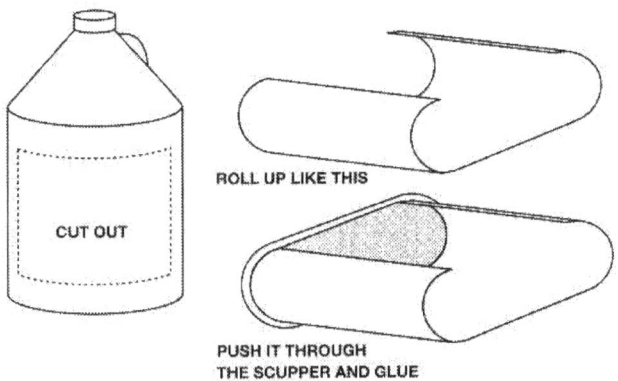

Figure 20
Scupper extensions are easy to make and keep dirty water from dribbling down the side of your boat.

We did find that the plastic bottle material becomes brittle after long exposure to the sun and eventually replaced it with white sheet rubber about an eighth of an inch thick. After searching in all the wrong places, we found that our local hardware store could order the sheet rubber. However, we had to go around twice to get the right thickness and flexibility. Scuppers vary in size and shape from boat to boat so you may have to experiment with thin pieces of cardboard until you have a good pattern to work with.

After Forty Years --- Dave Wheeler

Chapter Twelve
CRUISING BASICS

CRUISE PLANNING

Boats are different things to different people. They're a great place to spend the weekend, whether you go out for a ride, fix a few things or wash the boat. We know people who never take the dock lines off. They just keep working on their boats, rebuilding, refurbishing and adding new things. Some are fascinated with all there is to learn and take every boat course offered. Others spend their time and money installing the latest and greatest goodies. There's nothing wrong with any of these ways to enjoy a boat, but in my opinion, boats were made to travel the waterways.

Cruising has a magic of it's own. You see new places and meet nice people. Many become lifetime friends. You get to know the equipment on your boat really does work and you do know how to use the knowledge you learned in boating courses. A little serious cruising can give you something to talk about, but don't overdo it. One guy on our dock starts every conversation with how many times he's crossed the Gulf Stream and the number gets bigger every time.

The first step is getting away from the dock and that's not as easy as it sounds. There's an inertia that develops if you stay at the dock too long and it takes a few days to get you and the boat out of the dockside mode and into the cruising mode. A few things will probably go wrong when you start out, usually minor problems. The impellers in the pumps have been sitting there, bent one way, for a long time. If you haven't run the engines regularly, stuff settles in the hoses, shells grow on the intakes and the bottom may be fouled. A few shells on the props can destroy their ability to move your boat. That will create an embarrassing departure from the marina, if you get out at all.

Many of these problems can be solved beforehand. Have the bottom and the propellers cleaned. Thoroughly check out the engines. Change the fuel and oil filters and look at every hose clamp. Even if you have to pay a mechanic to come in, it will be far cheaper than having a problem later. As a transient, you'll pay list prices for parts and top dollar to a local mechanic you know nothing about. Clean out the pans under the engine so you'll be able to see any leaks and where they came from. If you're using dockside water, switch over to the onboard tanks and pumps a few days before leaving. Drop the anchor right at the dock and see if the winch will pull it up. Get out the hose and run some water in the bilges to make sure your pumps are working. All these precautions help, but on our boat, it's usually a few days before we really settle down and enjoy the cruise.

Planning a cruise carefully can make life easier. The plan will depend on how you want to travel. Most

After Forty Years --- Dave Wheeler

cruising boats are objective oriented. They have a goal, a place they want to get to and perhaps time is a consideration. A few lucky ones take their time, exploring and enjoying each place, changing their plans in a very subjective way. Even if you have to be someplace at a particular time, planning too long a day is an invitation to disaster. No wake zones, bridges and bad weather can make it a longer day than you thought. Arriving at a strange marina in the dark is an experience you won't like. Charts are cheaper than propellers and guide books can be worth their weight in bottom paint. It just doesn't make sense to skimp on buying any kind of basic information. A Triple A guide book will give you another slant on the town you're in, with more information on things like restaurants. People joke about having a road map on a boat, but if you're in an unfamiliar area and need parts, or want to visit someone, it might be useful.

There are some things you need to know before you get there. What marina or anchorage do you plan to stop in? How long will it take to get there? Does the marina have the depth or the power you need? Is there a big tidal range where you're going and how much water will you have when you get there? East Coast tides vary from nothing in some Intracoastal areas, to three or four feet in others and often more when the moon is full. What is the weather forecast? In the winter there are northers that may keep you from traveling. In the summer you may want to get up early to be in the next place before two or three o'clock to avoid thunderstorms. However, even with thorough research and meticulous planning, there are some things you can't be prepared for.

Bridges can be a problem, especially when you come around a bend and see one going down. Once in a while there's a communication problem. I call bridges on the proper channel 13 but sometimes they don't answer.

After Forty Years --- *Dave Wheeler*

When I check to see if they're on channel 16 and they still don't answer, I wonder if my radio is OK. In the St. Petersburg area, some bridges that go over the same body of water are hailed as "Structure E" or "Structure B." A little prior research with one of the guides makes life easier.

Marinas may not be what you envision from the guidebook. There were two marinas on the East coast, with identical specifications in the guidebook I was using. One marina had wide concrete docks with large pilings, brand new electrical outlets, a well-marked channel and a marine store with things you wanted to buy. The other one had old wooden docks, with two-inch spaces between the planks. The pilings may once have been fence posts--on a short fence. This outfit had a serpentine channel marked by PVC pipes and places in their channel that went bump on my bottom.

There's another great difference in marinas that isn't apparent until you get there. Some are primarily resorts or condominium developments and the marina is just one of their facilities. One place we visited wouldn't let us pay at night so we could leave early in the morning. They thought in terms of the rooms in their resort and wanted to be sure we didn't make any long distance calls or eat dinner in the restaurant. Another place had spent millions on pools and tennis courts for the condos, but the electricity on the dock barely kept a fan running.

Dockmasters vary. Some know very little about boats, but they've learned exactly what to tell you. Others can't deal with too many questions, like a waiter who recites a list of specials but is stunned if you ask him to tell you more about the fifth item. Girls with nice voices are very popular. Then there's the guy who's trying to sound like the Coast Guard. Some marinas just don't answer the radio at all. One place answered nicely, told us how to get in to the marina and assigned us a slip number. We never heard another word or saw anyone until we found the slip and went in to register. The service you get often depends on the dockmaster's situation. If it's a poor marina, he gets a lot of flack so he has an attitude to start with. The best dockmasters are captains or passengers who had to help on at least one long trip on the waterway. That guy knows about boats and your problems and he understands what you're talking about. That may not help much in a resort type marina if he's pretty low on the totem pole. The best place of all is a mom and pop marina that needs and wants your business, but there seems to be less and less of those.

If you did your homework first, checked out all the gear and didn't make an impossible plan, you can deal with these things. The result will be a beautiful cruise and a marvelous memory that will always be with you.

CRUISING FOOD

That's what we used to call hamburgers and hot dogs back in the years when we had those noisy cars and cruised through the drive-ins on Woodward Avenue. That was another life--now we're talking about boats and food to take with us on a cruise that might last several months. Although we have a freezer, a refrigerator and a microwave, we try to take a variety of foods that can survive without this equipment. At one "out island" in the Bahamas, our microwave was destroyed by a surge in the generator power and the first mate had to figure out how to cook all the microwave stuff in the oven. We always make an effort to save as much storage space as possible, so we seldom buy the large economy packages.

After Forty Years --- Dave Wheeler

Small boxes can be tucked in nooks and crannies.

ENTREES

Some friends recommended canned meats available by order from Brinkman's Turkey Farms. (16314 State Route 68, Findlay, OH, 45840, 419-365-5127). In addition to turkey, they have beef, pork and ground beef. We've always enjoyed their delicious meat and Jan makes a variety of meals based on these fine products. Lipton makes "Fast Cook" packages that include all the ingredients, seasoning and sauces. Most big markets carry a selection of these, plus many other brands. Lipton has an extensive line of dry, soup-based products, including Kettle Creations, Lipton Soup Secrets, Recipe Secrets and Cup-A-Soup. We also use Eggbeaters because my doctor suggested it but, honestly, I can't tell the difference, especially when Jan gets creative and makes omelets with them. World class cruisers say that eggs can be dipped in paraffin and stored for months without refrigeration, but I was never comfortable with that. Eggbeaters require refrigeration, but take very little space and can be stored indefinitely.

We're big on "Doggy Bags" and once in a great while, we actually give some to the dog. If the steak dinner was too big, take home the remnants, chop it up, put some packaged sauce on it and Voila!.. Beef Stroganoff. Almost any dinner can be reheated or rebuilt if it's kept cold or frozen. Pizza is good, (So it's loaded with cholesterol. Have another beer and forget it.) Taking home half a large pizza makes another complete dinner.

JARS, BOTTLES & CANS

Mark every can you buy with its contents and the date. If you lose a label, you won't know if you bought it last year or for that cruise seven years ago. Any can that has rust spots or bulges, should go directly in the trash. Canned foods with a high acid content should be checked often. There are many regular canned foods that make good dinners and are easy to make. Beans are easy to serve and practical. Canned fruit is good and usually popular with the crew. Spaghetti sauce, in sealed jars, lasts indefinitely and is delicious over noodles. We wouldn't think of leaving the dock without a major supply of peanut butter, although we always argue about creamy or crunchy. Another useful food item is Granola bars in a variety of flavors and ingredients.

VEGETABLES

Potatoes and onions last for months in a hanging wire basket. We've had good luck with bean sprouters, which are available at many health food stores. There are a variety of seeds such as alfalfa, mung beans, or whatever, but when you're in a far out spot and the lettuce has turned bad, these "greenies" will save the day.

BEVERAGES

One day, after our milk turned rotten again, we decided to try Parmalat milk. I'm not sure exactly what the process is but the package says it's not irradiated and no preservatives are added. It requires no refrigeration before it's opened but it has to be refrigerated after the package is opened and used within 10 days. We think it tastes fine and use it mainly for cereal and cooking. In fact, we haven't bought regular milk for a couple of years, whether we're cruising or at the dock. Most big grocery chains stock Parmalat. Tang orange drink works for us and contains many vitamins. We really prefer fresh orange juice but it doesn't keep very long.

Chapter Thirteen
AVOIDING MISTAKES

Many people don't realize when they're about to make a mistake and even the most experienced boaters get in a hurry. People are excited about their cruising plans and don't want to hear about possible problems, so we have bit our tongues and kept quiet more times than we should have.

OVER PLANNING

It's easy to get carried away with cruise plans. There are always more places that can be added to the trip and it seems silly to pass them by. As the itinerary expands, it can grow from a reasonable plan to an impossible dream. Commitments and dates when you have to be back can take the joy out of the trip. A tightly scheduled itinerary may force you to travel in rough weather and keep you out on the water for too many hours. When you get tired, your judgment goes downhill and you do foolish things. Long days result in late arrivals and a strange harbor after dark can be a bad place. No chart in the world has enough detail and no guide book can describe everything. Even if the dockmaster happens to be at the harbor after dark, it's virtually impossible to give an incoming vessel instructions exact enough to insure their safe arrival in the dark.

FRIENDS ON A CRUISE

People just naturally want to share a great yachting experience with their best friends, but it can be a recipe for disaster. Sharing a cruise should never be a spur of the moment decision. Think it over carefully and discuss details well in advance. Misunderstandings about sharing work create more bad feelings than anything else. Relationships are under pressure in close quarters, so it is important to really know the people you invite.

Guests either start out with you, or you have to meet them someplace. Your itinerary is then designed to accommodate the guests. If you have to pick them up along the way, you don't want to let them wait at the dock. Even if the weather is bad, you're committed to arrive at that place, at that time. If they arrive or depart by plane, you have an even tougher commitment, made worse if they have nonrefundable tickets. Make invitations with care. Pick people who know and understand cruising requirements and then make very sure your plans will be compatible.

CHECK ENGINES

Engines or generators do not self-destruct.

After Forty Years --- Dave Wheeler

Problems are almost always the result of little things that were not tightened or filled. If you don't look, you can't tell what's happening in the engine room. All fluids in both engines and the generator should be checked every day. After the regular checks, feel all the hoses and connections. If anything is loose, wet, or oily, check it out right away.

If your boat has been sitting in a marina for several months, starting out with a long run is a bad idea. Boats need exercise to stay in good running condition. Short runs on the waterway are the best way to check everything out.

LATEST CHARTS

One intrepid captain said he was just going on the ICW and certainly didn't need any charts. Another master mariner told me, "Hellfire, man, nobody's gonna move any of them rocks!" Not so. Builders are building, shorelines are changing, markers disappear and sandbars move around.

Get the latest word before you leave. It's embarrassing and expensive to find something did move. In view of the reduced number of updates being made by NOAA, it may be worth while to do a little research on the appropriate charts and notices to mariners.

ONLY GPS

Most boaters have had anxious moments when things look wrong and they are not exactly sure where they are. It happens, and unless you also plotted the courses in detail, there's no way to tell if something happened to your electronics, or if you put in the wrong numbers. An incorrect entry is easy to do with a string of waypoints. Your GPS or Loran gives course and distance from point A to point B, but it doesn't know what's between you and your destination. That line could go over rocks, or even through an island. Maybe those chances are remote, but it doesn't make sense to depend on any one system of navigation.

WAITING FOR GOOD WEATHER

This is the single most common reason people get into trouble, and if you're in big water, you can get into big trouble. Waiting to go offshore or start out on a cruise, it's hard to be patient. If you're in a marina and the bill is going out of sight, you really want out of there. If you have guests who don't know much about boating, it's hard to explain why you're waiting. Early morning conversation between macho captains out on the dock often sounds the same. One guy says, "Hey, it doesn't look too bad to me. What do you think?" The other replies, "Yeah, it might be a little rough but my boat can handle it." They keep pumping each other up until they go out on the wrong day and the Coast Guard has to go get them.

Check out all the possibilities before you leave. Experience may be a great teacher but it can be expensive and dangerous.

TAKING THE DOG

We've always had a dog with us. Every new port is an exciting experience and the dogs have loved every minute of it. They find interesting smells, bushes to kill, cats to chase and wonders to explore everywhere we go.

Obviously, dogs aboard require some special attention. If you head south where the weather is tropical, insects breed and multiply all year. In Canada, there are ferocious flies at certain times of the year. Mosquitoes in all parts of the country carry heartworm and regular preventive medication is necessary. Some mosquito repellents may not be healthy for your dog, but "Skin-So-Soft" diluted 50 percent will discourage the mosquitoes a bit. Ticks have to be physically removed and tweezers are the best tool. We've learned to pull the bug out parallel to the dog's body and not up at right angles. Try to get the entire tick out and don't get any of the blood on you, ticks can carry diseases. Don't try the old folklore trick of goosing the tick with a lit cigarette. It's a good way to burn the dog.

Figure 21
This rack holds the dog's water dish up off the deck.

We carry a Canine First Aid Kit, with Panalog for cuts, Benadryl, diarrhea medicine and Bonine for motion sickness. Be sure to check with your veterinarian for medications. Dosages vary for different sizes of dogs and some things that humans take are poisonous for them.

Fleas can be a problem. If the dog is not on one of the excellent flea treatments available now, a daily swim in salt water helps kill fleas. We hose our dog with fresh water after his swim, which he loves on a hot day.

Finding a good veterinarian in a new area can be a problem but we've had success asking other dog owners. If you have a purebred dog, call a breeder organization for advice. If you leave the country, a permit to import your dog will undoubtedly be required wherever you go. Be sure to check out all the requirements and write for information and applications well ahead of time.

A dog on a boat is going to fall in the water sooner or later. A collar on your dog puts a handle on the problem and a harness is not a bad idea for open water passages. It's easiest if you can lead the dog to a place where it can climb out. A swim platform on a powerboat helps but retrieving a big dog on a sailboat can be very difficult.

Our dog's water dish was a problem as it slid around on the deck. On teak decks water gathered under the dish and left an ugly brown stain, so we built a holder to keep the dish off the deck. Fasteners on both sides of the cockpit let us move the holder to the side, where it's out of the way.

Things do fall in and we keep a net handy at all times. Puppies carry their toys around and when we see them peering intently over the side, it's time to get the net. We don't mind if it's a tennis ball. Many marinas have tennis courts and the dog found every tennis ball ever knocked in the bushes.

Dolphin come alongside the boat and run with us. Noise makes them curious and we attract them by clapping. Our dog hangs his head over the side of the boat and watches for them. He gets so excited when they surface that we have to make sure he doesn't jump in the water. When he barks, the dolphin roll over on their backs to get a better look at the noisy animal. Our dogs are also fascinated by manatees. At ten to fifteen feet long and over a ton, they do get attention.

Kennel training is different for dogs on boats. In the Bahamas or northern Canada we're often at anchor. We tow an inflatable for trips to shore and one of our dogs had to be taken ashore several times a day, every day, in rain, storm, wind or whatever. He was trained on land and he simply wouldn't go on the boat, which created some tough trips to land in terrible weather. The dogs love the inflatable because they know it's their boat and the acting captain will take them to the beach where all that interesting stuff is. We trained the latest pup to "decorate the foredeck" and it's worked out very well. We wash the deck down at anchor with a saltwater pump. He refuses to use the deck when we're at dock because he'd rather go ashore where there are better things to see and do.

Some people let their dogs run loose in a marina or on the dock. That's like having someone else's dog on your front porch. When we walk the dog we always clean up after him.. There are very few marinas that don't allow dogs and we don't want to create any.

We've met people everywhere because of our dogs. They may be interested in the dog, or sometimes they have a dog at home they want to talk about. Our Dobermans were large dogs and some people were hesitant to approach them. However, when they learned how gentle they were, they got over it. One little girl got

Figure 22

Figure 23

Dolphin are special. They always smile and seem to like you. It may be just the way their faces appear but dolphin always look like they're smiling about some secret joke.

so carried away petting MacGyver that she fell into our boat. People all over the Southeast knew our last dog,

Gunnar. One day on the waterway in Florida, a lady on a boat going the other way, came rushing out of her cabin shouting, "Gunnar, where's Gunnar?" Then she finished putting her Bikini top on. The dog didn't pay much attention, but it sure made my day.

People often ask if the dogs get enough exercise on the boat. Actually, they get far more exercise than they did at home out in the kennel area. Now they swim every day and run for miles on beautiful Bahamian beaches or Canadian shores.

Our dogs wear collars with ID tags that have their name and "aboard Morning Star in the harbor." We hope that works for whatever harbor we're in but we've never lost a dog. In addition to the ID tag, they wear a rabies tag.

A dog of any size is an excellent alarm system which is good insurance at home, in a strange marina, or remote anchorage. We do take issue with people who talk about guard dogs. A determined villain can still overcome or outwit the biggest, meanest dog and we don't want that kind of a dog on our boat. Sometimes a little dog is more alert and makes more noise. I do have to admit that MacGyver occasionally chases away pelicans and seagulls.

People ask if our big dog is a problem on the boat. Sometimes it isn't easy to get around the dog when he's spread out in an inconvenient place, and no matter where we are on the boat, the dog usually has to come and help us. The size of the boat or the size of the dog doesn't really have anything to do with it. If we had a mega-yacht, the dog would still be right where he is -- just as close to us as he can possibly manage.

Figure 24
As you can tell our dog hates attention.

Chapter Fourteen
CRUISING THE ICW

THE RULES OF THE ROAD

It's important to know who's going where when you meet another vessel, especially in a narrow channel. The Rules of the Road cover almost any situation or type of vessel, the problem is, not everyone knows the rules or the correct signals. Even if you know the right moves, how do you know the approaching vessel has the slightest clue? If you want to really operate "by the book" it almost requires a "helm-chair lawyer" to get it right. There are rules for Coastal, International and Inland situations, as well as different rules for almost every atmospheric condition and type of vessel.

The Rules of the Road say that vessels meeting should pass each other by going to their right. That's the same way you would deal with an oncoming automobile on a narrow road. Basic whistle or horn signals are similar in most circumstances. Whether meeting or overtaking, one short blast means "I am altering my course to starboard." Two short blasts means "I am altering course to port."

When overtaking another boat, you must request permission to pass.

Incidentally, short blasts and long blasts are different. A short blast is one second and a long blast is four to six seconds, longer than most people pull on the lanyard.

If there's time, radio contact can provide an agreement that covers all the bases and there's no need to honk your horn. Some boats will respond to a call on the radio but very large vessels seldom answer and sailboat radios are often below, out of reach of the helmsman. Fortunately, there's a thing called the " Rule of General Prudence", which means do whatever you need to do to avoid collisions or problems. However, it's best not to get carried away with that one. If nothing else, a blast on the horn whether it's a proper signal or not, will get the other boat's attention.

Here are some procedures that have worked for us. First of all you have to assess the situation. Is there time to communicate? Is there a current involved? Current changes the rules because it applies force, moving a vessel downstream. The vessel moving downstream signals first and proposes a course of action because it is less maneuverable. Unless there is a substantial reason to disagree, the vessel traveling upstream must maneuver, slow down, or stop to enable the passage of the vessel being moved downstream by the current. Is the other vessel so large it could not alter course? Is there room to take evasive action? Our first move is a standard whistle signal to see what response we get. One guy tooted me a "shave and a haircut" and waved. The official answer is either repeating the same signal, or the danger signal of five blasts, meaning the captain doesn't agree or can't comply. If we're meeting head to head and there's time, I ease toward the center of the channel to give myself room, then turn sharply and momentarily to my right. The move is obvious and it doesn't require much interpretation. It usually gets the same response and we have two happy captains.

Sailboats take offense to a blast on the horn and may not respond to a call on the radio. I maintain my speed until I'm fairly close behind them and then cut the throttles back sharply. They almost always understand that reduction in engine speed means I'm a gentleman and plan to pass them slowly. Sometimes we do have a problem when they maintain their speed and their hull speed is about as fast as my trawler goes.

Everyone talks about the "ICW." There is no such thing. On any official sign or document, the proper name of the east coast waterway is the "Atlantic Intracoastal Waterway." Things are just as confusing if you go cruising on Florida's west coast. The inside passage from Fort Myers to Tarpon Springs is the "Gulf Coast Waterway". The "Gulf Intracoastal Waterway" goes from St. Marks, up in the Big Bend and continues around the Gulf to the Mexican border. So there's an AIW, a GCW, a GIW and no ICW at all. Whatever you call it, that remarkable trench from Marblehead to Marathon has given us some memorable moments.

We use radar and GPS every day on the waterways. The radar picks up thunderstorms, tells us which way they're moving and how strong they are. Several years ago, before we kept the radar on, we tried to beat a heavy squall into a marina. Unfortunately, it was a draw. Now we make the decision to go for it or drop the hook long beforehand. We also key in the coordinates of our destination for the day and the GPS constantly gives us a general idea of the distance to go without looking at the chart--we just have to ignore the warnings that we're fourteen miles off the course line.

I get a little upset when I'm right smack in the middle of the channel and the depthfinder shows shallow water. Maybe I only think I'm in the center. I check the markers on either side and then make a slow easy turn to one side while I watch the depth finder. If the water doesn't get deeper, I try it again to the other side. If none of the above works I just stay in the center of the channel, which usually works.

It seems that every time I have to refold a small craft chart, the wind is blowing, we're in a narrow curving channel, or a bridge is just ahead. That's when I reach the end of the chart section and have to find the matching part that says R-R on side B. It's sort of a test. You fold it, unfold it, turn the thing around and then right side up. I think the people who design these charts should have to stand on the roof of their building in a strong wind, unfold one of these charts and then see if they can find their Rs.

One day, while slowly overtaking a sailboat, a big yacht came around the bend ahead of us. It looked as though all three of us might arrive at the same place at the same time, which would not be a good thing. I kept watching, judging and waiting. We finally all got by each other and my first mate said, "Wow, that was close. Wasn't that girl something?" I replied, "What girl?" and she asked, "Are you trying to tell me you didn't see the naked girl in the cockpit of that sailboat?" Holy Moly! I don't know how I could have missed a thing like that.

After Forty Years --- Dave Wheeler

BRIDGES

Several years ago somebody decided to change the vertical clearance signs on bridges. Instead of showing a vertical clearance of 25 feet, the signs said the vertical clearance is 21 feet and in smaller letters below -- 25 feet at the center. That reduced clearance created a lot of panic, until people figured out what was going on. It still gives me a twitch when I see those lower numbers, which sometimes fail to correspond to those on the chart. Many tide boards at the side of the bridges are gone, beat up or so dirty they're hard to read and harder to trust.

Arriving at a bridge that's stuck in the down position is bad, at best. When sixteen more boats arrive and are milling around in all directions, I get nervous. One day, after a near miss, I got on the radio and suggested that when the bridge opened, no one would have to pass anyone else if the fast boats went first, cruisers second, trawlers third and sailboats last. Several people called back to say what a grand and reasonable idea. When the bridge opened, every single boat went flying toward the opening as fast as they could. So much for logic.

After Forty Years --- Dave Wheeler

After Forty Years --- Dave Wheeler

Chapter Fifteen
OBSERVATIONS

CHICKY ON THE BOW

Very few boats come into our marina without the standard equipment. They all have at least one engine, a VHF radio, a couple of fenders and a lady in a Bikini standing out on the bow, with either a line or a boathook in hand.

We're not talking about svelte swimsuit models or hot dog boats with thundering engines and lack of mufflers. Those boats with wild, jagged paint schemes on the side usually belong to some dude looking for his youth again, hoping the gold chains around his neck, the gold ring in his ear and exercise will help. These well-ripened Romeos NEVER have a lady out on the bow. His

After Forty Years --- Dave Wheeler

little piece of nonresistance is laying on the cushion at the stern, with a string bikini that's out of sight.

The ultimate chicky was on the bow of a sailboat at the Columbus Day Regatta, in Biscayne Bay. She stood there in an elegant pose, holding a glass of champagne, totally naked. Most chickies on the bow are a bit older, better clothed and on a little different boat-- usually trawlers or cruisers about 30 to 40 feet. The guy at the helm isn't exactly a kid, he wears a hat to cover his balding pate and a shaggy beard might be his most dramatic feature. Nobody even thinks "chicky on the bow." These are proud ladies caught in the Great American Dream. They're supposed to be out there. They stand there, a little uncertain of their footing, clutching a boathook or a coiled line, ready to spring into action -- more or less. Quite a few are a teeny bit chubby for a bikini, so they settle for swimsuits with flounces. Sensible shirts and shorts are not really acceptable. Some of them look downright annoyed, wondering how the hell they ever got into this situation. Others are very knowledgeable and know exactly how to throw a line. They can instruct the dockmaster that it's a bow spring and then point out exactly where they want it attached. A few get downright mean when the dockhand dismisses their instructions.

For most of those lovely mates, it isn't easy out there on the bow. Once in a while, we'd watch the fun if we were back in our marina early on Sunday night. Some of the returning captains had apparently been "over served", as they celebrated the weekend. The amount of shouting by the captain was in direct proportion to his embarrassment as he missed the slip and the boat crashed against the pilings. In the slips that were under big sheds, upright antennas made astonishing noises as they fractured and splintered. Screams of anguish added to the volume of sound as the maiden of the bow attempted to get a line on something -- anything at all, to save the boat and end the evening's show.

When Bayside Miami was Miamarina, a small powerboat came in. The gal on the bow was apparently going to throw a lasso over one of the pilings. The line was coiled and the loop was set. She stood there, knees flexed, in a stance like a black belt ready for the kill. Her concentration was absolute, determined to do it perfectly. As the boat approached the piling, the captain shouted, "now." She gave a mighty heave and the loop went six feet in the air and fell in the water. She'd been standing on the line.

A club in Key Largo has some slips for large yachts. On one visit we watched a smaller boat come in, maybe 40 or 50 feet. The captain pulled all the way into the slip bow first before he realized that they needed to get a line on the large single pilings way out beyond the catwalk. He discussed it with the lady at the stern, explaining that he wanted her to put a loop over those pilings when he backed up. They were rather high pilings, so his mate stood up on the transom to reach the top of the pilings. As he backed up, the wind took him to one side and just as she reached up with the loop, he gave the boat a quick touch of power to keep from hitting the piling. The stern moved sharply away from the piling but the lady didn't. She was left hanging on the piling -- but not for long. She slowly slid down the piling and into the water, while making a few observations about the captain, the splinters in her legs, boats and the joys of yachting.

One great couple had their own approach. They were at least in their late seventies and the two of them were the only crew on their 57 foot Chris Craft. They came in so quietly, we almost missed their arrival. As he brought the boat up to the dock, she hobbled out front and dropped the loop of the bow spring over a piling.

After Forty Years --- Dave Wheeler

Gramps brought the boat forward against that line, while his elderly mate tottered aft and dropped another loop over a piling at the stern. He left the engine nearest the dock idling in forward gear, while they secured all the other lines in a leisurely manner.

We made a point of watching when they left in a bit of a breeze. He warmed up the engines, then they tied a short and very tight line from a midships cleat to a piling right next to it. The boat couldn't move forward, backward or away from the dock. They took all the other lines off and Grampa got set at the controls. When he was ready, he gave the signal and Granma dropped off the last line. We've often used that technique and we call it "the granny line." Whatever their ages, the captain stayed at the helm, while his silver haired mate dealt with the lines.

The system is difficult to change. My first mate, Jan, is a well coordinated person and we decided she should learn how to run the boat and dock it. After one summer's trip, she was handling the boat very well. I talked her into bringing the boat in when we arrived back at our marina. I told her I had so much faith in her, that I'd take a line and go stand on the bow. We barely came through the marina entrance when people started shouting, "Look everybody, LOOK! Jan's bringing the boat in." They all crowded around the slip shouting advice, admonitions and a few remarks they thought were hilarious. Anyone would've had a difficult time docking under those circumstances but she made it. She handled it well, but we did learn a lesson. It's tough to buck the system.

BEARDS

There seems to be a relationship between boats and beards. My observations suggest that the length of most mariners' beards are in inverse proportion to the speed of their boat. Sailors grow the greatest collection of chin whiskers and, the older they get, the more hirsute they become. A goodly number of trawler captains also have beards, but theirs are more conservative and sometimes they settle for mustaches. Captains and crews on big yachts are invariably clean-shaven.

FILLING UP

I'm a freak about not running out of fuel. Somehow that seems like an incredibly stupid thing to do. My first mate and I had a regular system at the fuel dock. First I would gather all the necessary equipment; the tank wrench, a bottle of additive and a roll of paper towels in case of an overflow. I would pump and Jan called off the number of gallons, so I knew when the tank was close to full. She didn't call off every number -- maybe every 5 or every 10 gallons. One day a big gusher of diesel fuel came belching up from the fill pipe. It was in my face and soaking my hair. My watch was drenched and perhaps dying, when I called my wife. She didn't hear me at first; she was talking to some people. Ar-r-rgh!

NO WAKE SIGNS

While I watch the markers and the depth finder, Jan's job is to check out the "NO WAKE!" signs. These come in a variety of types. There's the standard sign that says, "idle speed, no wake", then below, it says the

After Forty Years --- Dave Wheeler

warning is for manatees but the channel is exempt. I've always wondered how they know not to go in the channel? There are speed restrictions for manatees from November 15th to March 31st. Do they have calendars? Some signs simply say "SLOW MANATEES." They can't be too darn slow if they stay out of the channels from the middle of November to the end of March.

Then there are the fake signs. Some have obviously been made by property owners, ranging from nice polite signs asking boaters to please slow down, to big angry signs with *"NO WAKE"* in bright red letters. The ultimate "No Wake" sign warns, "No Wake laws are strictly enforced by Sheriff Bobby Ray Teeter and offenders will be prosecuted to the full extent of the law." It clearly isn't an official waterway sign, but good old boys in cowboy hats and dark sunglasses scare me to death. I have the feeling that it might take a lot of time and money to prove I was right. The laws say that only official signs can be in the waterway. However, there are so many fake signs that enforcement is difficult or impossible. We've also been told that in one waterway neighborhood, the "Resume Normal Safe Operation" signs seem to fall down regularly. Keeping all the real "No Wake" signs up to date or replaced is difficult and expensive. The combination of fake signs, missing signs and unreadable signs is confusing. After miles running at five, knots the captains of faster boats begin to wonder if they missed the "Resume Normal Safe Operation" sign. Even worse, is seeing that sign after you've been flying along at top speed for a while.

Nobody in a "No Wake" zone is a happy camper. People with homes on the waterway paid a premium price for property that's being eaten away by an unending parade of boats. Powerboats run right at the speed limits -- and many are a teeny bit over it. Frustrated by the numerous "No Wake" signs, they want

After Forty Years --- *Dave Wheeler*

to make every legal knot they can. They usually turn on full power between the "No Wake" zones to make better time. Slower boats take a beating in those areas when a big wake maker roars on by.

The longer these problems continue, the less respect "No Wake" zones will get. Areas to be designated "No Wake" zones should be approved by an agency like the Coast Guard. Only approved signs could be displayed in the ICW. Printed lists of "No Wake" zones for the waterways could be available, like Notices to Mariners. Questions about "No Wake" areas would be eliminated. Vessels still disregarding the rules, should be prosecuted and home built signs featuring Bobby Ray Teeter would be unnecessary.

LOCKS

There are literally hundreds of locks shown on the U.S. Army Corps of Engineers Web Page, The river systems most used by private vessels include the Erie Canal, the St. Lawrence Seaway, the Mississippi River, the Okeechobee Waterway and the Atlantic Intracoastal Waterway. The number of locks in these waterways range from one in the Intracoastal, to twenty-seven in the Mississippi.

The St. Lawrence Seaway is international with big locks, big ocean going ships, big tides and big currents. The sixteen foot tide at the North Atlantic end is awesome. We spent a lot of time worrying about it, only to find that every stop had floating docks. We should have paid more attention to the current. The boat we had at that time could do 20 knots. The combination of the normal current plus a strong ebb tide, had us running near 28 knots heading to Quebec, where we planned to stop at the Quebec Yacht Club. When we spotted the club and made our turn, we wound up way past it. Coming home, the engines were running full bore to make 12 knots heading back up the river and we could chat with people fishing under the bridges. Suddenly, we knew why the guy in the little sailboat left at 3 AM.

Figure 25
Transiting locks requires the right preparation and procedures.

Transiting locks requires the right preparation and procedures. The moving water creates powerful forces and you may encounter huge ships in the locks. These are not a problem if you know how to deal with them. However, you can get in trouble if you are not prepared or fail to pay attention. Minor scuffs, broken rails or major difficulties await the unwary. A student in one of my Advanced Piloting classes was a tall handsome man with a shock of white hair and a far off look in his pale blue eyes. Those piercing eyes never quite focused on me, but appeared to be seeing past me to some far horizon. I don't know how much of the material he absorbed, but as time went by I learned he had bought a small freighter and dreamed of taking it around the world. He got as far as the Welland Canal, where he jammed that little freighter in the lock at an angle. He had to be pulled loose with a crane and the damage cost him enough to put his trip on hold for a long time. The following year, we started a new class and there were those blue eyes staring past me again. After the class I never heard any more of him. I hope he focused on the locks this time, instead of those far horizons.

Line problems in locks are common. If lighter vessels move around, they can damage themselves and others. The average length of dock line for a cruising boat is nearly equal to the boat's length. Much longer lines are required in a lock. If the lock is lowering the vessel, you can't get the eyes off bollards when you're 40 feet below them. The best approach is lines long enough to go from the boat up around the bollard at the top of the lock and back down to hand when the water is lowest. Make sure they are free and can be readily pulled down. If they jam, you just lost a line. Always consider the lines expendable and carry a sharp knife. If you get your hand caught, cut your line instantly. The forces involved are too strong and you don't have time to consider alternatives. Our locking lines are 100 feet long. In some locks, the Lockmaster may throw you lines attached at the top of the lock, but you should always have your own lines deployed in case they are not provided in the lock.

Basic preparations include protection for the boat. "Expert Beginners" may recommend bags of straw but the bags are often old and worn. They're seldom well packed and they get very thin between the lock walls and your gunwales. Many lockmasters will refuse to let you use straw bags because straw can get in the inlets and outlets if the bag breaks. Some locks have smooth steel walls and others are rough old concrete or broken limestone blocks. All lock surfaces are slippery and slimy. Some of the barges use old tires but they'll really mess up a white hull. Another folk story suggests holding empty, aluminum cans at the end and using them to push off from the wall. Don't do it-- the cans get bent out of shape and they slip easily. Some locks have ladders with metal rungs that you can hold on to, or double a line over in a gentle lock. We wear heavy rubber gloves with textured surfaces, both for pushing against the wall if necessary, and protecting our hands as we let the line run through.

Your best bet is very large fenders. One boat had huge ball shaped fenders, which worked well, but they rolled easily and were hard to keep in place. Standard fenders should be vertical and watched every minute to keep them positioned correctly. There is great difference between the water currents in locks. Some are very powerful, creating strong surges boiling into the center of the lock and making your boat hard to handle. The Lockmaster can control the water flow and sometimes does so in rough locks.

We found that the locking process takes at least half an hour per lock if there is no waiting. If there are several locks to go through, the time should be included in your travel plans. We were put through the Welland Locks with a Canadian Destroyer. Military vessels are given priority and we moved through rapidly. Unfortunately, we started late in the day and entered Lake Erie in a rainstorm at midnight. The long steel breakwall of the town next door led us in by showing brightly on our radar. After securing our boat, we broke out the bubbly that night. We went through the St. Lawrence Seaway locks one time when the Canadian Lockmasters were on strike. They made us wait at each lock for hours, until instructions came over the

After Forty Years --- Dave Wheeler

loudspeakers in rapid fire French. It kept us from getting to Montreal and we spent a night tied to a lock wall. I think we had a few drinks that night as well. Locks can expand your range of travel, but they must be used with respect.

After Forty Years --- Dave Wheeler

Chapter Sixteen
INFLATABLE DINGHIES

BOTTOM PAINT

Inflatables gather appalling amounts of seaweed and aquatic creatures. It seems to happen instantly. Actually, most people get busy doing other things and leave the little boats in the water too long. When we finally got to it, we usually had to work all day scrubbing the bottom with 3M scrubbers soaked in Clorox and water. Often, we had to use the blunt edge of a flexible plastic scraper designed for spreading epoxies or resin. It was a long and ugly job. Tom Ebbert at Curtis Marine in Key Largo, suggested we use Muriatic Acid, slightly diluted, on our 3M scrubbers. We were a little afraid to use it but Tom told us that if we didn't get it in our socks and kept the inflatable rinsed off, it shouldn't be a problem. It worked like a charm.

This year we found a jet black bottom paint for

use on inflatables. It's Number 1855 Aqua-Clean, made by Petit. It comes in a kit called "A to Z", that includes the paint, a can of #15045 bonding agent, plus a spray nozzle and a pad of bronze wool. When I discovered that it was water based, I almost gave up on it. Maybe it would wash off? The can was so heavy I assumed it had some kind of metal in it and the label said it contains over 58% cuprous oxide. There are explicit instructions -- two coats are required and the paint must dry thoroughly before putting the boat back in the water. Leaving for the Bahamas in a week left us no time to experiment. We used it on the bottom. When we returned three months later, the paint was still on and there was, virtually, no growth on the bottom.

STOWING GEAR

There are a lot of things you *want* to take with you in the inflatable and the Coast Guard says there are a lot of things you have to take. Horns, flashlights, a copy of your registration, (a ziplock bag is good), repair stuff and miscellaneous gear that rolls around inside the boat. We found a totally waterproof bag developed for white water rafters. It was the solution to keep everything in one place and dry. On soggy days my wallet and watch go in there too.

INFLATABLE FLOORBOARDS

Inflatables are great dinghies. They're stable, don't scratch your boat and are easy to move around. Different makes and designs have a variety of floorboards, but the plywood floorboards in some of the older ones were a disaster. Some manufacturers use cheap varnish that comes off immediately. New varnish comes off nearly as fast and scraping the residue off is a major project. Some of the newer inflatables have an epoxy base finish on the floorboards, and even though it's a much sturdier finish, we found that nonskid tapes or finishes didn't adhere to it very well. The best inflatables have floorboards made of plastic materials.

We took the old wooden floorboards to a furniture stripper and had them completely cleaned off. After a light sanding, the first thing to go on the floorboards was a thin coat of liquid epoxy. Since the wood is totally clean, the epoxy will soak deep into the wood. Sand that coat very lightly to avoid cutting through the epoxy and destroying the seal. This is a case where smoothness is not as important as protecting the wood. Most of the brush marks will be covered by the final coats of paint. An epoxy base paint will adhere best to the sealer coat and a color that matches the inflatable will make the job look professional. Petit's EasyPoxy works well and is available in appropriate colors.

Epoxy paints have a high gloss and can be slippery. After the paint is completely dry, we mask off about four inches all around the edges (so the boards will still slip into place) and then apply a nonskid coat that creates a much safer surface when you step in with wet feet. Epoxy paint with nonskid added, will give you good adhesion and is easy to keep clean. Make sure you use white nonskid, because black will soak up the sun's heat and blister your feet.

INFLATING THE INFLATABLE

Most manufacturers supply a bellows type air pump that takes a long time to do the job, especially if you want the recommended amount of pressure. An inflatable air gauge will show you how much pressure is actually in there. It's quicker to put the initial air into the inflatable with an electric air pump. However, they do have a limited capacity and we've found that the final pounds of pressure have to be added with a foot pump. You'll be disappointed, as well as sweaty, if you do all that pumping in the hot sunlight. The inflatable will get flabby as the air cools down and contracts. Pump it up solidly in the shade or in the evening. After it's in the water, it's a scary experience to remove a plug and try to quickly get more air in the boat before it sinks. Let it sit overnight, and if the inflatable is soft after the sun shines on it, you have a leak. A little soapy water will pinpoint the leak but it takes some careful work to get a leak perfectly sealed from the outside. There are a surprising variety of fabrics and they all require a special kind of glue. On small leaks, we've had more luck with Inflatable Boat Sealant made by Inland Marine. Take out the air plugs momentarily and pour in the sealant. Before it dries, turn the inflatable upside down, on its ends, on its sides and every way you can think of, to get the sealant well distributed.

CRUISING WITH AN INFLATABLE

An important concern is to get it out of the way when landing the big boat. In a slip, the dinghy will have to be at the bow or at the stern and at a long dock, it will have to be alongside. While the captain is handling the big boat, the first mate will have to deal with the dinghy. Often you can call the marina on the way in and ask where you will be docking, so you can put the dinghy in the right place.

After Forty Years --- Dave Wheeler

TOWING AN INFLATABLE

In an area like the Bahamas, where anchoring is sometimes the only choice, a dinghy is a vital piece of equipment. If you lose it, you're in real trouble. In remote cruising spots, it's impossible to buy another one, which could end the cruise, even if you're many miles down island.

In our first attempts, we tried using two separate lines. Our idea was that if one should break, we'd still have an inflatable. Completely separate lines were a disaster because the dink refused to tow in a straight line. We solved the problem by fastening the two individual lines together. Each line has a stainless snap hook for the towing eyes low on either side of the inflatable's bow. The other ends have loops for the cleats on the big boat. The two polypropylene lines were about the same length as the big boat. We laid them out on the dock and about ten feet from the dinghy end, fastened them together loosely with a black cable tie.(Black ones last much longer than the white.) We don't tighten the ties until we are sure the two lines are the same length. Around ten feet from the transom, we bound them together with another cable tie. Then we divided the remaining line into even parts and fastened the lines together with cable ties. Each of the lines were still separate and intact, but now formed a single towline with a bridle at each end. When a test run confirmed that the dinghy towed properly, we went back and tightened up the cable ties. There was some excess material to trim off the ties and we cut the ends of them round so the sharp corners don't hurt our hands when pulling in the line.

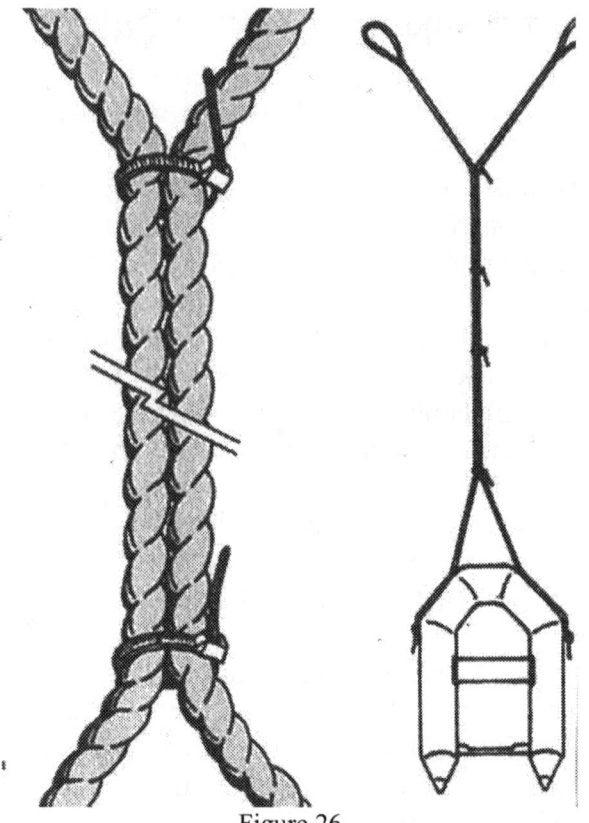

Figure 26
A doubled towline with both ends spread like a bridle.

We elected to use polypropylene for towlines because it has surprising strength and it does float. However, don't get too confident that polypropylene will always stay on top of the water and away from your propellers. Always pull the dinghy up to the boat and stow the line before you jockey around with the anchor. If any part of the line is close to a propeller when you're maneuvering, it can get sucked in no matter how well it's supposed to float. Take my word for it--cutting wrapped up line off the shafts will definitely ruin your day.

Sunlight will weaken polypropylene. It should be

kept out of the sun and checked often for deterioration. We flake the line down into a milk crate as we pull it in, which minimizes tangles, and then put a life preserver cushion on top to keep the sun off the line.

We feel so confident with the double towline that we now put our motor on brackets on the stern and tow the inflatable across the Gulf Stream, instead of stowing it on the big boat tied down.

THE DINGHY AT ANCHOR

At anchor, we used to let the dinghy trail out behind the boat. We used two lines about twenty feet long, with snaps for the dink on one end and loops on the other end for our transom. When they were in place, they formed a V from the transom to the bow of the dinghy, which rode nicely in place and stayed with us even if one line should come loose. However, we had problems with the dinghy trailing behind us. In strong winds, it gets little protection from the boat and one overturned in a storm. That was not healthy for the outboard. At night, a dinghy out away from the boat is also a tempting target for thieves.

Some boats can tie the dinghy behind the boat across the swim platform, with a line to each side of the transom. It's easy to get in or out, but it may rub against the edge of the swim platform. We've seen several approaches to this problem. One was a piece of heavy plastic hose, sliced from one end to the other and slipped over the edge of the platform. It was tough to cut it right and we never found a good way to secure it that didn't have screw heads exposed.

We came across a type of fender that is designed with a built in groove so it can be kept on a stainless steel railing. With some muscle and a touch of Vaseline we forced one onto the edge of our swim platform but it didn't stay on very well, even tied. We then tried one hanging fender about 6"x18" and balanced the dinghy on it, with lines at either side of the transom. Although it was better, it slid up or laid at an angle. The final solution was adding a six-inch piece of 3/8" anchor chain to the bottom of the fender with a shackle. We do have to clean the chain now and then but it hangs straight and it does the job.

LOCKING THE DINGHY

We worry a lot about securing the dinghy when we're in the Bahamas because it would be difficult to replace over there. We always lock the motor on the dinghy and, in some places, lock the dinghy fast to the boat. The length of the two cables used will depend on your situation but be generous, because it's better to have some slack than not enough. We use 3/16" stainless cable because it's more intimidating and a little harder to cut than the 1/8" cable. A two inch loop will work in the 3/16" cable and a thimble isn't necessary. After the first loop is swaged tight with oval sleeves and a swaging tool, a piece of garden hose is slid over the cable before the other loop is put in. Pull the first loop tightly into the end of the hose so you can make both loops close to the ends of the hose.

Locks can be a problem. We've tried brass and plastic enclosed locks but they all have steel parts inside that rust. You must keep the lock literally soaked in oil, because when you can't open the lock, you have to cut the cable. I have to admit to making very long cables and gradually making them shorter as I cut off the cheapest locks I could find.

GETTING INTO THE INFLATABLE

Getting out of the water and back in the dinghy can be a struggle. We scrape ourselves on the hardware along the top and I've lost my trunks trying to slither over the pontoons.

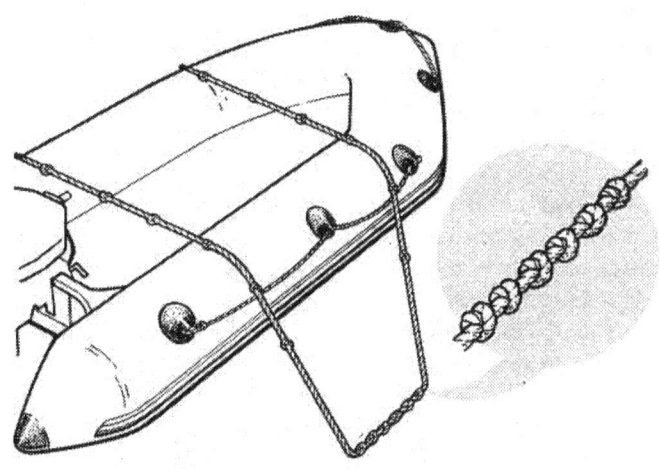

Figure 27

Dinghy boarding step.

Last year we found a solution for that problem. It isn't exactly a rope ladder, but more of a rope step that helps you get your body high enough to get over the side. We double a piece of line, three eighths of an inch in diameter and about 20 feet long and tie a group of knots in the center. The knots can be fancy or simple and create a step you can feel underwater with your foot. They're also easier to put your weight on. Put a simple knot every six to nine inches up both sides. These are just to give you a good grip as you pull yourself up. We then added a strong stainless snap to each end of the line.

When we're out snorkeling, the line is snapped to

the side opposite from where we plan to board. We have lifting rings about four feet apart on each side of our inflatable and these make strong attachment points. The lines come across the dinghy, over the opposite pontoon and hang down in a V about three feet long on each side. That group of knots is at the bottom of the V, and by stepping on the line, you can boost yourself over the top with a little less pain and embarrassment.

Chapter Seventeen
SAFETY

CHECKING THE LIFE JACKETS

Think about it -- in an emergency, how long would it take you to get a life jacket out, put it on and fasten it properly?

The Coast Guard no longer talks about Personal Flotation Devices (PFDs) because most people think of them as life preservers or life jackets. The Coast Guard believes that people should wear life jackets at all times. That may sound excessive but in a crisis there may not be time to get a life jacket out and fastened. Single hand sailors or fishermen out by themselves should always wear a life jacket. Over 800 people fall overboard and drown every year. Sixty percent were not wearing life preservers. Putting one on in the water is difficult or impossible. If you think you're in such great shape that life jackets are not important, you're wrong. The more physically fit you are, the less buoyancy you have because fat helps you float.

Dig out those life preservers and check them out. Are they covered with mold and mildew, or old and beat up? If they're Type I jackets with blocks of Kapok and have air leaks, throw them away because the Kapok probably lost its buoyancy. Never use a life jacket for a cushion and never put one away wet. The Coast Guard says there should be life preservers or life jackets readily accessible for every one on a boat. Even if you meet that criteria and have the approved life jackets on board, it doesn't matter at all if you can't get them on and properly secured. Life preservers must be fit to each person by setting all the straps and fastenings properly. They aren't much help if they slip off. For children, check the fit by picking up the child by the shoulders of the PFD. If they fall out, tighten the straps. Each member of your family should have a custom fit PFD, printed with their name in an indelible marker. After the fittings, head for a swimming pool and see how they work. Lay back and see if you're still floating. That might be more important than you think, because swimming with a big Type I jacket and floating is difficult.

Following are official types of PFDs, with a few unofficial comments.

Type I -- Offshore life jacket

These jackets are preferred by the Coast Guard for offshore use. These PFDs provide 22 pounds of buoyancy but they're big, bulky, hot and not very comfortable to wear. However, if you fall overboard unconscious, it will float you face up, which is rather important.

Type II -- Near shore buoyant vest

Not as bulky but with slightly less buoyancy. These are still not comfortable for warm days or working but they may still turn you face up.

Type III -- Flotation vest

Most comfort for continuous or working wear. These are aids for swimmers. Many styles are available.

Type IV -- Throwable Device

Cushions, rings and horseshoe buoys come under this category. Be careful not to hit the person you're trying to help.

Type V -- Wearable special use device

Although not as safe, these are approved for special uses and are easier to wear for extended periods.

Type II vests and Bib/yoke styles are preferred for infants and small children. All boats, 16 feet or longer, must also have a throwable device in addition to the required PFDs. There are even Coast Guard approved products like children's swimsuits in bright neon colors, with encapsulated kapok blocks. Once these suits are put on, they can only be removed by an adult.

FIRE EXTINGUISHERS

All extinguishers have labels with instructions that are not very informative. The extinguisher type is designated by a letter enclosed in a circle, a triangle or a square. Obviously, everyone on a boat should know these symbols and their proper use. One extinguisher with B and C symbols claimed it should never be used on a class A fire of combustible materials. That created an uncomfortable vision of looking up symbols and reading labels on the extinguishers to find the right one to use while the boat burned. That isn't going to happen. A person discovering a fire will grab the nearest extinguisher and try to put it out. Most labels say "the units should be checked monthly and must be installed, inspected, maintained and tested in accordance with the Standard of the National Fire Protection Association titled Portable Fire Extinguishers." Say what? A recent Boat/US article reported tests on a number of older extinguishers, most of which hadn't been out of their brackets since being installed. There are also labels put on by local companies, indicating the last date the extinguishers were inspected. The dates may indicate that the unit is long overdue to be inspected, while the gauges at the top show the pressure is still satisfactory.

Many labels have information that make little sense to most people. The label on one of my extinguishers states that it was tested to ANSI/UL 711 and ANSI/UL 299. It also says it's TYPE USCG TYPE A SIZE II TYPE B:C SIZE I. No commas and also says it's no good unless bracket number MVCP-5 is used. What? It had thirty four lines of instructions about installing, inspecting, maintaining in accordance with NFPA standards and detailed information on how to recharge it. Even if I could find out where to get the chemicals, the instructions were definitely beyond me. Maybe I need a copy of "Fire Extinguishers for Dummies."

The Halon unit in our engine room had some interesting information. This unit was state of the art when we installed it--an automatic Fireboy, Model

After Forty Years --- Dave Wheeler

100VH with Halon 1301. This label was much better, it simply said that the owner should read and comply with the installation instructions and the owner's manual. It says the extinguisher should be weighed every six months and if the weight falls three ounces below the correct weight, it should be removed immediately and returned to the dealer or the manufacturer, labeled as hazardous material. However, I couldn't find anyone who ever weighed a fire extinguisher. Weighing is more critical with Halon bottles because many models did not have pressure gauges. Extinguishers with Halon replacements now have pressure gauges.

The content of these labels should be simplified. Codes are useless unless everyone knows what they mean. The person who spots a fire may be a guest. Big letters that say PAPER, FABRICS AND WOOD -- FUEL, SOLVENT AND GREASE or ELECTRICAL would be more useful. Regular maintenance that must be done should be stated emphatically and clearly. Long-term maintenance can easily be forgotten. It should be possible to simplify some of the more confusing labels because Coast Guard regulations are now based on test criteria that all portable fire extinguishers must meet.

Several organizations publish standards. The National Fire Protection Association publishes marine, as well as residential standards and will sell you a copy of their NFPA 10 marine standard for $35.00. The Coast Guard Equipment Approval Office in Washington, makes their product decisions based on tests by several independent laboratories. Underwriters Laboratories are major players in the marine area and are, in fact, the prime testing organization for most Coast Guard Fire Extinguisher Standards. You can buy copies of the individual requirements from the UL and their technical experts will discuss any particular questions with you. The American Boat and Yacht Council is primarily involved with boat builders. Their minimum annual membership is $75.00 for an individual. If you join, you may then buy their book of standards for $125.00. I asked a respected captain how he learned what the requirements were. He said he never did know but the boat dealer assured him the vessel was properly equipped with the correct fire extinguishers.

The basic types of extinguishers now available are Dry Chemical, Carbon Dioxide, Foam and Halon substitutes such as FE-241 and FM-200. Every fire extinguisher is categorized and labeled by type and size. An "A" in a triangle means the extinguisher should be used on materials like paper, wood, fabric, rubber and some plastics. A "B" in a square indicates an extinguisher for flammable liquids such as gasoline, cooking oil, grease, solvent and paint. A "C" in a circle is shown on an extinguisher for live electrical fires.

Extinguishers can be activated manually or with temperature sensors. The hand operated portable extinguisher can be quickly moved to the flames but has the disadvantage that if the fire is in an enclosed area, a door or hatch has to be opened, allowing additional oxygen to feed the fire. The official classes of hand portable units are B-I and B-II. Ratings might be expressed as 1-A; 10-BC, or 3-A; 40-BC. The numbers relate to the approximate square feet of that category fire that can be extinguished. For example, an extinguisher classification 3-A; 40-BC means that unit will extinguish a class A fire of combustible materials about 3 ft square and the 40 BC part means that it should deal with 100 sq. feet of fire generated by flammable liquids or electrical sources.

None of the above means much unless the extinguisher is aimed and applied to the fire correctly. Generally speaking, the extinguisher has to be aimed at the base of the flames. Even if you have to "waste" a small extinguisher, practice putting out a test fire in a safe area ashore. It won't cost anywhere near as much as a real fire aboard.

    Coast Guard studies indicate that 90% of marine fires start in engine compartments. Temperatures exceeding 165 degrees activate automatic systems. Automatic units are available for a wide range of areas from 75 to 1000 cubic feet. These sizes encompass spaces from 5 foot square and 3 feet high to about 13 feet square by 6 feet high. The chemical in most automatic fire extinguishing systems will not shut down diesel engines and the agent may be exhausted through the engine before the fire is extinguished. For that reason, diesel powered vessels with automatic fire extinguishers must have automatic engine shutdowns. Automatic units are also available with a back up manual discharge in addition to the heat activation. Audible alarms are recommended with the automatic systems because an engine room fire may not be apparent. I can attest to that. On one occasion, I had no idea a generator fire had started and been extinguished while I was running the boat from the flybridge

    Dry chemicals work by smothering the flame, depriving it of oxygen. Smaller units are relatively inexpensive and it may be most cost efficient to simply replace them. Units of this type range from about fourteen to seventy five dollars, according to size. The only maintenance an individual can do on a dry chemical unit is to turn it upside down to make sure it hasn't solidified. Dry chemicals are now being made with silicon type additives to eliminate caking. Some of the larger dry chemical units can be refilled.

    Foam extinguishers work by blanketing the flammable material and not allowing oxygen to feed the flames. They are very effective for fires fed by liquids like fuels and solvents, but should not be used on electrical fires. They're uncommon primarily because they make a major mess.

Carbon dioxide has the advantage that it leaves no residue to clean up and the gas will not cause harm if it is taken through an engine. Most units dispense a 40% concentration that replaces the oxygen to a point that it cannot sustain fire. Few CO2 extinguishers are used today. Compared to the FE-241 extinguishers they are larger, heavier and more expensive. Their state of charge can only be checked by weight.

Halon has two major problems. Halon 1301 has an extremely high, ozone depleting potential--16 times the ozone depleting potential of the outlawed Freons. Most boat builders have now switched to FE-241. Halon does not extinguish flame by oxygen depletion, but by chemical reaction. Halon in an extinguisher is at a low concentration, around 5%, and displaces only a small percentage of the oxygen. Therefore it will continue to be discharged through the still running engines and the fire will not be extinguished. Existing Halon systems are "grandfathered" and do not have to be immediately replaced, but an automatic engine shutdown system must be installed for it to be effective. An audible discharge alarm is highly recommended.

The CG Recreational Boat Office at 1-800-368-5647, is one of the best sources of information on requirements. They will send you the information at no cost, answer basic questions or turn you over to their technical experts. The Coast Guard Auxiliary will be glad to give your boat a Courtesy Examination, including your fire protection equipment. Chapman Piloting, Seamanship and Small Boat Handling has good coverage on the subject.

After all the research, it turns out that the actual Coast Guard requirements are very simple--perhaps too simple. The only specifications are for B-I and B-II hand portable extinguishers, even for vessels up to 1000 gross tons. To give you an idea how minimal these requirements are, a one hundred thirty foot Hatteras yacht, at 294.3 gross tons, needs only three B-II hand portable fire extinguishers aboard to be legal. The Coast Guard has no requirements for fixed automatic fire extinguisher systems in engine rooms.

Regardless of the size of your vessel, the requirements are not unduly difficult or expensive to meet. However, there are more important criteria than the official standards. The knowledge that your vessel is properly equipped should be a matter of pride. In the final analysis, your investment, your life and your family's safety require a level of protection you can live with.

I've talked with many experts in a variety of organizations. Regardless of regulations, requirements or standards, there are some basic elements that should be included in your fire protection plans. Prevention should be the first consideration. Where could a fire start? Are there any conditions that would strengthen a fire if one started? Are these "hot spots" accessible with fire extinguishing equipment? Engine rooms, with heat, fuel and volatile fumes require particular attention. Paint lockers and galleys have grease and solvents that are highly flammable. Another dangerous element is electrical wiring. Electrical fires start with sparks, poor connections and hot overloaded wires.

The next most important consideration, is getting a portable extinguisher to the fire. An extinguisher close to hand is vital. Walk through the boat and ask yourself, "If a fire started here, where would I get an extinguisher?" Locating an extinguisher may be a compromise between availability and having the unit in the way, or possibly in danger of being set off by accident. The weight of the unit and how well it can be moved, handled and aimed is also important.

The type of extinguisher should be appropriate for its location. An extinguisher in a forward stateroom should have an A rating for fabrics and combustibles. It would seem reasonable to have A and B-C on every extinguisher on the boat so the extinguisher is good for all possibilities. The proper rating for a galley is B, to deal with grease and flammable liquids. Dry chemical units are the most common types on a boat. They're very effective and although they cover everything with a dry chemical powder, a big mess is better than a big fire. The powder problem can be avoided with portable CO2 or Halon 1211 units. Both of these extinguisher types are heavy and expensive. Halon 1211 is no longer in production but some companies do reclaim existing agent.

Fire is the greatest danger for any open water cruiser. Out at sea, there are no fire departments and no one to call that can respond immediately. You cannot survive a fire unless you or the equipment aboard can put it out.

Chapter Eighteen
NAVIGATION

On navigation articles, many magazines require a disclaimer as follows. It may sound like ducking responsibility but it does make some good points.

Directions, distances, or coordinates are for planning purposes only. All directions are magnetic and all distances are in nautical miles. Loran settings may not agree between different kinds of equipment and GPS accuracy varies at government discretion. Some charts are not perfectly accurate. They may not have been updated recently, or they may not have the detail necessary for good positioning. Any coordinates may vary because the source has a different interpretation of the position. For example, Off Bird Key, 300 yards north of Bird Key, approaching Bird Key, or Bird Key Light may or may not be the same place. Anchorages may not be as stated. New laws or physical changes may make that spot unsuitable. In the final analysis, the navigation and safety of your vessel is your own responsibility and the prudent mariner never relies on a single piece of information.

THE COMPASS

Today's electronic navigation instruments border on miraculous. We can run little cars on Mars or put numbers from satellites into tiny boxes that guide us to an exact spot on unmarked waters. Computer navigation programs are commonplace and chart plotters are competing with them. Those electronic marvels have been around for quite a while, but they've never replaced the compass. A Chinese emperor, Huang-ti, put the first one in his chariot in 376 BC. Today, over two thousand years later, every well-found vessel still has a compass.

That old magnetic compass is a basic instrument on every boat. It may have competition from a variety of electronic systems, but it's invariably right there in the middle. It needs no electric power and it indicates directions even if the vessel is stationary. (Electronic systems show a course only if the boat is in motion.) If all else fails, you can go around the world with a compass and a watch, just as many great explorers have done. Entering the wrong numbers in an electronic navigation system can put you on the rocks. If you're vigilant and your compass is working properly, you may notice that the compass doesn't agree with the other displays before errors create serious problems.

Today's compasses are more complex than the original magnetized needle floating in a bowl of oil, but the principles are the same. Long lived permanent magnets, low friction or jeweled bearings and special clear oils that float the card and reduce excessive motion contribute to greater accuracy. A new configuration is the fluxgate compass. Two electronic coils sense the magnetic field of the earth. The readout is digital and can be sent directly to other electronic devices. Like the magnetic compass, fluxgates are subject to deviations. Many units are self-compensating to deal with deviations. The compensating process is based on the rate of change which should be consistent as the vessel rotates. If the rate of change increases or decreases, the internal program inserts a correction, or compensation. To minimize deviations, the sensing unit can be placed anywhere, far away from magnetic influences. Fluxgates do require electric power and they must be level. Sailboats use fluxgate compasses mounted in sophisticated gimbals to deal with heeling angles.

The globe we live on is the power source for magnetic compasses. Those forces are like an enormous bar magnet in the center of our planet, aligned approximately with the geographic north and south poles. All magnets have positive and negative poles and a magnet floating freely will align itself only one way with that theoretical bar magnet in the center of the earth. If you label the correct end of the floating magnet as north, you've got a compass.

The floating disc in your compass with the directions on it is called the card. It rotates on a pivot and has graduations showing directions. The card has magnets on the bottom side and it's partially supported by the fluid in an enclosed bowl. The floating compass card turns freely inside the compass housing. It appears to point to North, West, or various directions as it turns.

THE CARD DOES NOT TURN. IT POINTS STEADILY TO THE NORTH AS YOUR BOAT TURNS.

Obviously, the compass has to be installed where

you can see it and work with it and perhaps even sight over it for rough bearings. Sun can damage the clear top, so it should be covered when not in use. Compasses have a "lubber line" or a white indicator peg fastened to the housing at the most forward edge of the card, which should be the side away from you. The graduation on the card closest to this peg indicates the direction of the boat. A line projected over both the pivot point of the card and the lubber line must parallel the fore and aft center line of your vessel. Preferably the compass will be directly on that center line. It should also be clear of any magnetic influences.

Two things modify compass readings. They are variation and deviation. The terms may sound intimidating, but it's easiest to remember that:

In most instances, a combination of both variation and deviation will be present and the resultant compass error will be the algebraic sum of these two elements.

VARIATION is caused by the fact that the north and south magnetic poles are offset from the true north and south poles. It is essentially the angular difference between the directions of the geographic and the magnetic poles. It changes with your geographic location. Variation is relatively constant and every published chart indicates the amount of local variation. There are local anomalies created by different densities in the earth's mass or local materials that change the magnetic field. On a cruise to Quebec, we found that the Canadian charts for Kingston, Ontario, warn that local magnetic forces vary so much that it would be unsafe to depend on a compass for directions.

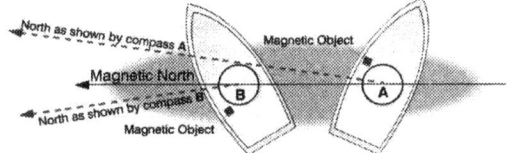
Magnetic objects on the boat and close to the compass cause deviation.

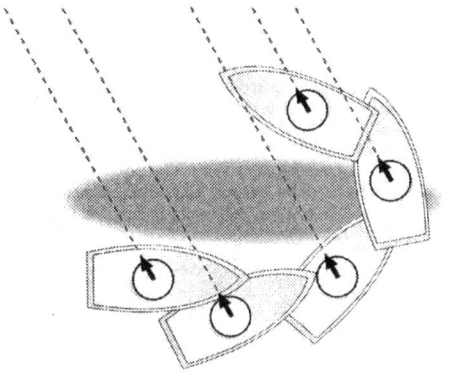
Swinging ship a good way to figure deviation and correct it by adjusting the compass magnets.

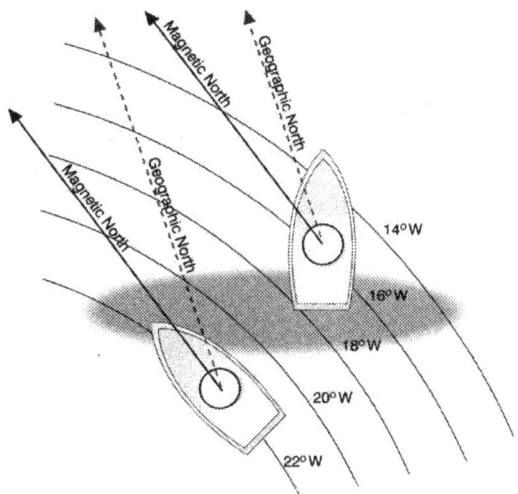
This drawing shows the difference between magnetic and true north, or variation.

Figure 28

VARIATION is caused by things OFF the boat.
DEVIATION is caused by things ON the boat.

After Forty Years --- Dave Wheeler

Variation is shown on the compass rose, a graphic device on the chart similar to the compass card. The compass rose is the connection between the direction shown on your compass and the directions indicated on your chart by courses or bearings. The rose usually has two separate circles showing compass directions. The outer circle indicates the direction of the geographic North Pole, termed the true direction. On Mercator charts, true directions are parallel to chart latitude and longitude lines, which are aligned with the earth's geographic north and south poles. The inner circle shows directions as they are modified by magnetic variations in the area. Those differences are stated on the inside of the rose. For example the directions inside the rose might show that a compass will indicate north to be so many degrees left, or west, in a given year. It will also show that this difference increases or decreases by a certain number of minutes each year. The later information is very important with DMA charts that may be over ten years old. For example, Bahamas chart number 26306 shows a variation of 5° 11' west for 1985 and an annual change of 8' west. That means that you have to add twelve times the annual change which is 96' or 1° 36' to the 1985 variation of 5° 11.' The total, or 6° 47', is the difference between a true direction on the chart and what the compass should indicate. Corrections to west variations are added and corrections to east variations are subtracted. The memory device of "West is best and east is least" will help remember which one should be added.

The compass will still not indicate the right direction if there is any deviation. Remember, deviation is caused by things on the boat. Anything made of iron-based metals near your compass will attract the magnets in your compass card and make it point that way. Magnets of any kind nearby will really make the compass crazy. One of our boats had a flybridge and my daughter thought it would be cool to pipe the stereo up there. She kept after me until I ran the wires up top and built in a couple of speakers. They were excellent speakers and I soon became aware that they had BIG magnets. The music was great but my compass wasn't. Then I was in serious trouble convincing my teen-age daughter that the speakers had to go.

Deviation changes with the boat's heading. As the boat turns, the compass card tries to continue pointing to magnetic north, but the card is deflected toward the magnetic objects on the boat. What you observe is the resultant (the algebraic sum) of two forces, magnetic north and magnetic objects on the boat. The differences would be difficult to memorize because they change on every heading. One approach is to make a deviation table that is simply a list of the differences between what the compass says and what it should say. You can determine those differences, or deviations, by a technique called "swinging the compass."

Be sure that the compass is zeroed before you start. Most manufacturers do zero their compasses but if you have any doubts, you can check it out yourself. Take the compass off the boat to an area free of any magnetic influences. Turn the compass until the lubber line points to north and mark that heading on the surface where the compass is located. Now revolve the compass 180° and the lubber line should be exactly at south. If it isn't, use a nonmagnetic screwdriver to remove half the error of the larger (EW or NS) error. Turn the compass 180° and remove half the error again and continue removing half errors until all the error is removed.

You'll need help and a nice day to swing the compass. One person maneuvers the boat, holding the compass to an exact heading while crossing a range line. A second person marks and records what a pelorus says at the instant the boat crosses the line. A columnar pad is ideal for recording the readings.

Using a single range and a pelorus is the most common procedure. Landmarks you can see that are also shown on the chart make good ranges and give you more working room. A half mile is best. The Light Lists show accurate ranges. Don't use buoys as they're floating around on the end of a chain.

If necessary, calculate the magnetic heading for the range.

A pelorus has two sighting blades that rotate over a compass rose. It should be positioned with the north/south line parallel to the keel. A clear view in all directions is necessary.

Steer the boat at angles across the range in a series of courses by compass headings 15° apart

On each run, the actual heading of the boat (as opposed to what the compass shows) is determined by sighting the pelorus and marking the heading when crossing the range. For example, the range may have a magnetic heading of 106°. The pelorus may read 110°, 96° or something similar. Each run is recorded as read and then all the pelorus readings are averaged. The result might be 103°.

The difference between each of the individual pelorus readings on the range and the average of those readings, is the deviation.

The next problem is to modify the compass readings, or compensate for the differences. Almost all compasses have internal compensator magnets installed at right angles, for East-West and North-South adjustments. The deviations can be eliminated by the adjustment of those magnets. External magnets called Flinders bars can be placed around the compass in such a way that they correct larger deviations and in more extreme cases, deviations can be neutralized by installing two masses of soft iron abeam on either side and equidistant from the compass. Devices of this type are called Quadrantal Correctors.

The most common method of compensating the compass requires running reciprocal courses out on the water. A quiet day without wind or current is important. Run a steady course on a cardinal point, either 090° or 270° from a landmark or fixed marker and then turn 180° and run the opposite, or reciprocal, course. If the compass reading is not exactly 180° different, use a nonmagnetic screwdriver to remove half the error with the appropriate screw (NS or EW). Only half the deviation is removed, because after a 180° turn, the deviation shown is the total for both headings. You may have to make a trial turn of the adjusting screw to find which way removes or adds degrees. Continue to run the same two courses, taking out half the error each time until the deviation is either gone or reduced to the smallest possible amount. Follow the same procedure on the other two cardinal points.

Compensation can also be done with the shadow of a pin in the sun. In this case, winds and currents are not a problem, but a sunny day is necessary. The runs can be shorter but the process has to be completed before the sun moves too much. The basic tool is a compass card with a vertical pin in the center. Start out on a cardinal heading such as east and rotate the compass card under the pin until it reads east, or 090°. Make a 180° turn and the compass reading should come around to 270°. If it doesn't read correctly, use the same method of reducing the errors by half until all error is gone. Repeat the process on the north and south headings.

People ask if you can compensate a compass with GPS. Out on the ocean, currents, winds and constant corrections made by the GPS make it virtually impossible. On a longer run across the Gulf Stream, it's evident that the GPS is leading you through a series of curves, but the same thing is happening on shorter runs. On a large inland lake with no current or wind of any kind and perfect steering, it might be possible to correct a compass with GPS. The lake would have to be large enough to make a fairly long run. Loran might be the best bet. Even under perfect conditions, setting up the courses and their reciprocals and steering the boat perfectly, would be difficult.

The other common question is: Why fool around with the compass when you have GPS and Loran? First, the compass always works, whether you have power or not. Second, the GPS only knows where you have been, telling you the average of the directions you've traveled and comparing that with the computed destination. It doesn't know whether the resultant course goes through shallow water or over an island. To me, because I've been there, the compass provides an instant and constant comparison between the heading, based on the numbers you entered and the direction indicated by the compass.

Heavy commercial vessels or military vessels may be required to change or shift cargoes of large metal masses, making it impossible to compensate compasses because of the changing deviations. Most of these heavy vessels are built of steel, adding to the difficulty of compensating the compasses. In these cases, the deviations may be recorded as a set of reference numbers or on a "deviation rose", which is simply two roses, one inside the other. The differences for each are shown by drawing a line from the magnetic courses on the inside rose to the compass course on the outside rose required for that heading. A traditional and elegant solution to larger and irreducible deviations is a "Napier diagram." This is a standard form on which the deviations are plotted. It creates a smooth curved line that will show any discrepancies in the recorded deviations. It also allows you to interpolate between the plotted points and convert between magnetic and compass headings.

Give that compass the respect it deserves. A correctly compensated magnetic compass is an independent device that doesn't require external power. Underway, it becomes part of an onboard piloting system that doesn't need to receive outside information. It provides a constant cross-check on all other navigation equipment. It's foolish to put your boat at risk by depending on any single navigation system. The foundation of all navigation is charting, piloting and dead reckoning. The compass is a basic part of those functions.

CARTOGRAPHY

One beautiful morning, we left the Sassafras River at the north end of Chesapeake Bay. The boat was running perfectly, our course was plotted on the latest chart and all seemed right with the world -- but it wasn't. At first, we noticed that a few of the channel markers had strange numbers and suddenly, none of the markers or buoys matched anything on our chart. We hadn't changed course but nothing around us made sense. Totally disoriented, it felt as though we had slipped into a time warp or had developed some sort of mental problem. We fumbled along at idle until we finally saw the big bridge down by Annapolis. Later, we learned that most of the buoys in the northern section of Chesapeake Bay had been moved or renumbered and we didn't have the latest Notices to Mariners.

Those notices are critical as markers are moved to accommodate changes in channels, new developments and demands from the increasing number of people living on the waterfronts. You can call the Coast Guard headquarters for your district and get on a mailing list for

After Forty Years --- Dave Wheeler

the Local Notices to Mariners. It isn't easy to manually update charts even though the instructions in the Notices are clear. Finding each and every specified marker and each coordinate is tough on the eyeballs and takes a long time. Many mariners do not make those corrections properly or in a timely manner. Several organizations and new chart producing techniques now offer the notices in a variety of formats that are easier to work with, but many mariners had so many problems in the past, they tend to avoid it.

Ancient navigators traveled the coasts using known landmarks and sailing directions from other mariners. They had little interest in venturing out of sight of land and possibly falling off the edge of the world. Only 100 years ago, there were still people who refused to believe Joshua Slocum had circumnavigated the earth because they still believed the world was flat.

In those early times, charts didn't exist and mankind was limited to about one quarter of the planet's surface. Any real exploration had to be on the oceans where the surface had no recognizable points of reference. Map making was then based on measurements to or from objects that could be seen. Between 1676 and 1793, the Cassini family of famous map makers, first used geometry based on visual points of reference. However, out at sea there were no structures, hills or highways; nothing was in sight but the stars in the sky. Early navigators did use the most prominent stars to guide them but it was hundreds of years before celestial navigation came into general use. Other than walking, animals provided the only transportation and that ended at the water's edge.

Monarchs pressed for continuing exploration hoping for treasure and power. Monks drew charts based on sketches from explorers, hearsay and imagination. Many of those charts were illuminated and had marvelous illustrations of fantastic denizens of the sea. Conquistadors were sent out to search for gold and slaves. In later centuries, whaling ships explored far corners of the earth, searching for their giant prey, while commercial vessels took their trade to foreign shores. Conquest and commerce forced continual improvement of charts and the printing presses of the world supplied the need.

I taught Advanced Piloting for several years and always made the point that new charts were cheaper than running gear. I also emphasized that Notices to Mariners provided critical information. Things do change. New developments move shorelines. Artificial reefs and assorted materials are dumped in the waters and create new obstructions. Storms erode the beaches, sand moves someplace else and creates a sand bar..

Famous explorers ran aground constantly. They checked depths with a lead line and moved ahead slowly. Ships still foundered because lead lines only show what's directly below, while the greatest dangers are ahead, under water and out of sight. That put many of Spain's galleons of gold on the bottom. Fleets of treasure ships left Havana and headed directly for the Florida Keys, an area of deadly reefs that still holds many treasures, now grown over with coral in Florida's sanctuaries and forever untouchable. Those ships wanted to use the Gulf Stream current to increase their speed, but navigators of that time had only a few sketches for charts. A few had sailing directions or notes from others who had made it through the area. Captains distrusted the navigators and insisted on courses that included sighting *good solid points of land* to establish the vessel's position. They reasoned that even if navigators miscalculate, land doesn't move. Over fifteen percent of ships traveling past the Keys were wrecked on the reefs by errors in navigation, bad weather or pirates.

After Forty Years --- Dave Wheeler

Early coastal navigation was based on the direction of prevailing winds or prominent headlands. Timepieces were rare or nonexistent and hourglasses were time limited and easily broken. John Harrison invented the first marine chronometer. It wasn't approved by the British government until 1765. The magnetic compass was first seen in European and Mediterranean waters in the fourteenth century, although it had existed in the Orient at least 200 years before. It was, and still is, the basic navigation instrument used on ships at sea. The log, a device dragged through the water, was able to provide information about the ship's speed. The basic elements of dead reckoning -- speed, time and distance, still required someone to go out there and either fall off the edge, or find out how far it was to new destinations. That required at least dedication and courage, if not a touch of lunacy.

The success of the explorers varied. Some were successful, but they all had marvelous stories to enhance their reputations. A few brought back gold and jewels that galvanized acquisitive monarchs. Charts improved as more explorers were sent out to search for treasures. At first, the rulers thought in terms of "rape and pillage," but it wasn't long before they realized they could add provinces and colonies to their kingdoms.

Whaling ships and conquistadors found new corners of the world to chart. Marine cartography became a priority, and the printing press made charts more available than ever before. Prince Henry, of Portugal, was responsible for major advances in navigation. Matthew Fontaine Maury, a U.S. Navy officer, made systematic studies of the oceans and their currents. He also started uniform methods of reporting weather at sea and is considered the father of modern day pilot charts. Benjamin Franklin crossed the Atlantic several times with the express purpose of mapping Gulf

Stream currents. Captain James Cook is known for his explorations of the Pacific and many charts resulted from his travels. Nathaniel Bowditch wrote the tome, "The American Practical Navigator," that became a bible for mariners.

The First World War introduced many questions about marine charts. People in aircraft were the first to look down on the surface of the oceans and the earth. It became evident that not every island on the charts were shaped or located correctly. The growth of shipping and air travel put more emphasis on marine cartography. World War II forced more changes in charts. Submarines needed to get around underwater. New electronic devices painted pictures of the bottom that didn't exist before. By the end of World War II, charts were greatly improved. Military, commercial and private mariners came to expect that all charts would be exact and updated regularly.

The number of people involved, rising printing costs, and the operation of ships actually dragging a wire across the bottom, made the production of marine charts extremely expensive. Nevertheless, the process was funded by the government without question for decades. Mariners were appalled when NOAA finally increased their prices.

Searching for ways to save money, many people opted for books of charts. Even though the books included some unwanted charts, and could cost up to a hundred dollars, all the individual charts would have cost far more. Some companies offer exact copies of NOAA or NIMA charts. You must specify precisely what original charts you want copied. The copies are in black and white. I imagine color is possible, but would probably be very expensive.

NOAA is the National Oceanic and Atmospheric Administration. The National Ocean Service, or NOS, is part of their organization, and the Office of Coast Survey is a branch of the NOS. The Marine Charting Division works with both these offices. The DMA, or Defense Mapping Agency, is now the NIMA, or the National Imaging and Mapping Agency and is part of the Defense Department. Imray-Iolaire is a private company in England that publishes charts of the eastern Caribbean. The name, British Admiralty, is still commonly used for charts from the United Kingdom Hydrographic Office, which is undergoing changes.

The Office of Coast Survey is now the agency responsible for charts. They have an inventory of nearly a thousand charts for United States waters. NIMA publishes about eight thousand charts for the rest of the world, and nearly half of the annual production from both organizations goes to the military. Critical, high traffic areas of our oceans that have not been surveyed in decades still exceed 40,000 square nautical miles. The time is hard to find and fund, and reduced budgets have been blamed for cutting NOAA's survey fleet from eleven ships to three.

Designing a marine chart is more difficult than making a map of land surfaces. It is not only a fluid medium and three dimensional, it varies with time. The mariner needs to know about tidal and current information, as well as the configuration of the bottom. Protocols are required to define the levels of multiple and changing surfaces. Sea level, depths at low and high water, and heights above those water levels must be stated in an agreed upon manner. There are objects overhead to be measured in an agreed upon format, so you will know how much room exists at a particular tidal height, or more succinctly, whether your mast will get under that bridge. Current can obviously move you off the line you plotted on the chart and perhaps into a shallow area. Spherical surfaces and long distances create major problems for marine cartography. Try stomping a basketball completely flat and the problem becomes evident. There is no perfect way to reproduce a convex surface on a flat surface.

The three most commonly used projections, or mathematical systems, are Polyconic, Gnomonic and Mercator. The Polyconic projection is used in the Great Lakes and Inland bodies of water. Land masses are shown quite accurately, but courses over distances may have errors because the lines of longitude curve toward the poles. The Gnomonic projection is designed with spherical geometry for the purpose of providing a curving course that compensates for the earth's curvature, to provide the shortest distance from A to B. However, land masses are extremely distorted by this projection.

Only one method is named for an individual. Gerardus Mercator's first cylindrical projection of a world chart was published about 430 years ago and that projection is still used more than any other system. It creates great distortions in Greenland and Antarctica, but there aren't too many voyagers in those areas. Using Ptolemy's concept of latitude and longitude grids, the meridians are parallel and intersect the latitude lines at right angles. A direction anywhere on a Mercator chart can be measured in degrees from the grid lines. Distance can be measured from the degrees shown on the right or left edges of a Mercator chart because one minute equals one nautical mile.

The 1988 congressional decision that our charts must be changed to metric is still unofficially on hold. We're currently the only country in the world making charts with depths in feet and fathoms. In addition to the number of charts that would have to be totally redone, many American captains would surely change them back to feet and inches, just to be sure they won't go aground.

As demands to balance the national budget

increased, the government became less sympathetic to the expense of producing marine charts. The Marine Charting Division is now fully computerized and all NOS charts will be updated using computer technology. Computer techniques have cut the time to design, revise and produce a new chart, from eight months to two months. NOS is now producing more new editions per year than ever before.

In the past, you called the Coast Guard headquarters for your district and they put you on the mailing list for the Local Notices to Mariners. NOAA is now working on weekly electronic updates. They plan to put all corrections in an electronic patch, available to subscribers via the Internet or on disks. Those corrections, such as repositioned buoys or obstructions, can automatically modify the chart shown on the navigator's computer screen and are applied directly to new paper charts printed by the Marine Charting Division. I believe Canada was the first to simplify updates long before anyone else. They still make corrections with small sections that paste right over the old information.

Another important document, available at no cost, is the "Dates of Latest Editions." It's important to know whether the chart you're using is the latest edition, or has been replaced by a new one. Another element is chart datum, which is simply a group of agreed-upon references for one point in time. Surveyed features on a navigational chart are positioned on a horizontal datum system such as NAD27 (the North American Datum of 1927) or NAD83 (North American Datum of 1983). In addition to horizontal datum, all charts require a vertical datum. It's important to know whether the information from the Global Positioning Satellite is the same as the Chart Datum you're using. In non-tidal waters such as the Great Lakes, water level and chart datum elevations are referenced to IGLD 1985 in cooperation with Canada. (International Great Lakes Datum 1985).

Private companies won the right to print, publish and sell charts several years ago. Chart Kit published books of charts, and soon began to produce computer disks that could hold hundreds of charts. These are CD-ROMs, which means "compact disk-read only memory." A CD can easily hold an entire encyclopedia. Twenty CDs on navigation, tide tables, charts or related marine information, would fit in a space 7 1/2 inches long, by the disk container's size of five by five and a half inches. It would be difficult, if not impossible, to find enough room on a private vessel for all the charts, books and information those disks contain.

Today, virtually any chart you may want to use is available on a CD-ROM. There are programs that enable you to use those charts to plan and plot out your next cruise. Many combine both digital charts and navigation software tied into the Global Positioning System. There are elegant programs providing tide and current information that can be integrated with navigation or charting programs. You can track your boat's progress in real time, including the effects of tides and currents. The Nobeltec Visual Navigation Suite includes tide bars and current arrows, over 100 planning charts, interaction with autopilots and depth sounders, and a direct link to the Internet for the latest information.

GPS is no longer degraded for private use. Combined with the Coast Guard system of "Differential GPS" navigation, accuracy is phenomenal. I marvel when my GPS tells me to turn at a discrete point on a featureless open sea. I've learned that when my GPS says "close", I better look ahead immediately or I might hit a marker. Courses plotted by GPS alone provide the distance and direction of a straight line from A to B, but that line may go through shoal water or an island --

After Forty Years --- *Dave Wheeler*

which is not a good thing. Today, there is great concern about the many new captains who have not had learning experiences such as running aground. They are traveling on the surface of the sea using nothing but numbers from those metal balls in the sky.

The "POD" system stands for "Print On Demand." Major book publishing companies also use this system. It eliminates printing new editions or keeping large inventories on hand. NOAA plans to update the digital files of all its charts every week. The files alone would be sent to selected agents, allowing them to instantly print any chart you request with information no older than one week, including the latest "Notices to Mariners" plotted right on them. The same file updates can automatically bring disks of digital charts up to date. Mariners can even request that specific routing and waypoint information be included on vector charts. The plan is to provide customized charts, available on demand, at an estimated cost between ten and fourteen dollars.

Marine navigation is being redefined. Millions of mariners are now using digital charts and navigation programs. Crusty old salts, as well as novices, have embraced this new level of navigation. It's what's happening. If you don't believe that, rent a car with a GPS mapping system in it. Be prepared for a voice to tell you, "Sir, you have just passed the turn. Go two blocks further, turn left and follow the new instructions." Mariners are also making new turns. Cartography on sea and land has changed forever.

Chapter Nineteen

COMPUTERS

ELECTRONIC CHARTING PROGRAMS

If you're planning a long cruise using electronic navigation, order the paper charts, too. Think about it. If you spent $500.00 for paper charts, $1000.00 for an electronic charting program and several CDs covering entire regions for $250.00 each, it could come to two or three thousand dollars. That may sound like a lot but the cost of running aground makes anything you spend for charts and programs insignificant. Towing alone could cost you a minimum of $125.00 an hour, plus $10.00 per foot of the boat being pulled off. Damage to the bottom of your boat or the running gear can run into big bucks and, if you damage a reef, the numbers are astronomical.

By all means go electronic, but some basic knowledge about navigation will make the navigation programs work easier for you. When you select a chart, it usually comes up zoomed in on a particular location. Then you have to zoom out to find the destination and the chart you want. Printed Chart No.1 will make it easier to pull up the right chart numbers on the CD when your destination is close to a line between charts. Also, make sure your compass is compensated before you leave. If your compass and your navigation program don't agree, you have a problem. Having said that, the best system of all is a combination of electronic navigation programs, with background knowledge of the "old time" navigation. Together, they provide extensive information, in addition to faster planning and plotting- and one is a check on the other.

Figure 29

Paper charts will orient you when using electronic chart programs and are necessary backups.

Over the past decade, the development in

After Forty Years --- Dave Wheeler

electronic charting programs has been extraordinary. Today raster charts outsell paper charts by 8 to 5. In this age of computers, genomes and nanotechnology, the consumer has come to believe that technology might possibly be good.

Virtually any chart in the world is now available in a digital format. You can plan, plot and monitor your next cruise in real time with navigation programs. They combine the charts with navigation software tied to the Global Positioning System. GPS signals are the keystone of electronic navigation programs, and now that those signals are no longer degraded, the combination of GPS, differential GPS and WAAS results in pinpoint navigation accuracy.

Today's navigation programs provide an astonishing range of information and options. There are too many to list all of them, but some of the elements are average speed, bearing to next waypoint, course up, north up, cross track deviations, distance and bearing to a waypoint, distance and time to the destination, distance traveled, elapsed time, estimated fuel consumption, ground track, instant latitude and longitude, speed over ground, tide and current data, true and magnetic course and velocity made good to a waypoint. That's one long, list and there's no way in the world you can keep all those computations up to date with a pencil, or even with a calculator.

Always make sure you have the latest chart CDs. It's just as important as it was with the paper charts. There are the early BSB charts, CHS and NDI Canadian charts, Jeppesen RasterPlus hybrid charts, bottom contour charts, Maptech International raster charts, Nobeltec Passport world vector charts, Photo Navigator charts and Softchart Nautical charts.

Companies that produce digital navigation programs now compete by adding additional features.

After Forty Years --- *Dave Wheeler*

Tide and current data are integrated with many navigation programs and the vessel's progress is tracked in real time, including the effects of currents. Digital charts may be combined with radar, underwater and aerial views. Touch screen activation and programs to monitor video cameras, are available. Weather programs can be automatically tailored to your cruise plans and shown on your screen. There are also several independent weather programs with worldwide coverage. Photography, charts, radar and bottom contours can work together to provide a multifaceted picture of your vessel's situation. The future may bring more changes like interactive voice operation, instantaneous translations in other countries, multimedia charts, or even virtual reality views of harbors that resemble an arcade game or a flight simulator.

Raster and vector are the two basic types of charts available. A raster chart is based on a grid of horizontal and vertical lines or coordinates. It is essentially a picture of a chart produced by digitally scanning a paper chart. A raster image file is very large because it identifies each of the coordinate intersections to illuminate in monochrome or color values. A raster file is a list of those dots, or bits, commonly referred to as a bitmap that creates the picture of the chart. They are easier and less expensive to produce.

A vector chart is a database that contains a point-by-point representation of a chart. It can be magnified greatly and remains sharp at all zoom levels. Vector chart formats were first made available to the boating public on chart plotters. A new program uses a hybrid raster-vector presentation. Vector charts can be instantly modified with layers to remove or add information such as markers, notes or updates from Notices to Mariners. That ability enables you to temporarily remove information so the details you need are easier to see.

After Forty Years --- Dave Wheeler

These charts have faster panning and continuous zooming. The screen color schemes can even be changed to meet the captain's preferences. Vector charts are more difficult to produce, but easier to change. A vector chart is a collection of data that can be selectively modified.

None of this is pertinent unless you can see the details on your computer screen. The number of pixels, or the number of discrete dots available to create an exact and usable image, describes computer screen definition. More pixels provide a better quality image displayed on the screen and better printing capabilities. There are two common LCD technologies for laptop computers, active matrix and passive matrix. Active matrix is brighter and has better contrast. This is important where bright sunlight can make a monitor unreadable.

Flat panel screens are creating great changes. It started with laptops but now flat screens apply to PCs as well. Flat panel displays are significantly brighter, and feature higher contrast than traditional CRTs (cathode ray tubes). They have contrast ratios from 200:1 to 500:1, which means these screens will work well in boats even if sunlight shines in the pilothouse.

The best programs do what you want quickly, easily and intuitively. Even the best will be better if you have a basic knowledge of charts and charting. Take some of the available boating courses. Don't start out with one of the most complex navigation programs. Take a little time to work at home with one of the planning programs and gain some experience plotting next year's cruise. Find the charts you need to display, and experiment. Start by establishing your point of departure and the coordinates of the first place you plan to go. Set up the course and, if that course line goes across land or shallow water, add another waypoint that takes you around it. Study the chart and you'll see more information about that first course, such as adjacent markers or landmarks and the bearing and distance to the next waypoint. As you get familiar with the program, you will be able to call up information on local tides and currents, current weather information, speed and fuel usage, or even a contour map of the bottom you're traveling over. In any case, before you buy anything, talk to experts or visit a retail outlet that will let you have a hands-on experience with these systems.

If you plan to use one of these programs, find a computer with these minimums: a high capacity hard drive (30-60 megs), 256 or higher memory, 1.5 gig or faster processor and a stable operating system such as Windows XP.

Laptop computers can be located on the helm where they're easy to see. Remember that installing and removing charts can leave debris on your hard drive such as unused registry entries that may eventually create problems. Some programs include uninstall options and others should be handled through the add/remove system. The combination of these programs and a basic knowledge of navigation can take you anywhere in the world with confidence and safety.

THE INTERNET

E-mail is fast becoming a system someplace between CB and the long sought lingua franca. It is so ubiquitous, that the United States Postal System may go bankrupt. They admit that constantly raising prices cannot solve their problems. It is impossible to write a letter and take it to the mailbox or the post office that begins to compete with the speed of E-mail. You can keep in touch with friends, or even order parts sent to the Shangri-La Marina.

One fascinating characteristic of electronic mail

is lauguage translation, which enables correspondence between people anywhere on earth. You can order a widget and later learn it's coming from Hong Kong. Ideas and attitudes are being blended. No one knows what you look like unless you send him or her a picture. Correspondents may be black, white, yellow, red or someplace in between. Religions may be different and objectives may be anywhere from information retrieval to criminal. It may, indeed, change us all to some degree.

SEARCH ENGINES

There is no encyclopedia that can compete with today's search engines, even if the encyclopedia is on a CD and can be used on your computer. I can ask Google anything from metric equivalents, to insect types, to stem cell research and get 74 choices of each in an instant. People are using search engines to learn about everything, and ordering an increasing amount of products online. They make personal choices from the details of the next camera or car they want, to the demographics of a town where they might want to live.

After Forty Years --- Dave Wheeler

Chapter Twenty
SECURING THE BOAT

Cruising will take you many different places and a variety of places to "park" your boat. It's important to be sure your boat is securely and safely moored, whether you're at a dock, on a mooring or at anchor.

THROTTLE BALL

Our first powerboat seemed much more complicated than the sailboat. It had two engines and many controls. On our first cruise up north, my wife and I were both on the flybridge as we approached the dock. I didn't know the boat was still in forward gear when I grabbed a throttle instead of a clutch. I shoved what I thought was the clutch into forward and my wife flew off the bridge into the cockpit. Fortunately she wasn't hurt, only bruised a bit, but clearly upset. She was still able to make a few suggestions about my boat handling and they weren't necessarily helpful.

I was frightened and embarrassed by that incident. Since then, the throttle balls on our boats get special treatment. I remove them and screw them on to a dowel to use as a handle. Then they get painted with a liquid epoxy. While the epoxy is still sticky, I roll them in a paper cup of fine gravel or the coarse sand sold for bird cages. Nonskid additives will work fine, but the bird gravel is rougher and scratchier. After they dry, I paint them with a bright red epoxy paint. The objective is to make them instantly recognizable and clearly different than the smooth black clutches. Now there isn't any question, I know which controls are which without looking at them.

Figure 29

Throttles are red but a coat of paint with a textured surface or a different shaped knob will stop you from using the wrong handle when backing or maneuvering.

After Forty Years --- Dave Wheeler

HOW PROPELLERS WORK

Good landings require balancing the forces affecting the movement of the boat. Wind and current are the prime external forces to consider. The mass of the boat, the shape of the hull and keel plus the water pressure as it passes by the hull, keel and rudders are factors to be worked with. Propellers and rudders are the primary tools that can compensate for the sum of the forces involved.

A single engine boat normally has a right hand propeller. Even with the rudder centered, when the control is shifted into reverse gear, the stern will walk to port because the thrust from the individual propeller blades is unequal. A propeller screws itself through the water, creating a corkscrew motion with the discharged water. The blade moving upward pushes water up and outboard, as well as to the rear. This creates pressure against the hull and an opposite force against the propeller, moving the stern to port. The downward moving blade has little effect because it pushes water away from the boat.

Twin screw vessels have counter rotating propellers that counteract each other, but the same forces come into play when the propellers are used individually. In addition, the props on a twin are well outboard of the center of the vessel and that increases their leverage. These are the basic elements to remember. Forward on either engine starts the bow to the opposite side. Aft on either engine starts the stern to the opposite side. Forward on one and reverse on the other rotates the boat. Backing the boat works the same way.

After Forty Years --- Dave Wheeler

DOCKSIDE CONNECTIONS

We have fun watching how people secure their boats. One thing we've noticed is the way people deal with docklines. Most know that in tidal waters the eye of a mooring line should be on a dock cleat or over a piling, so the lines can be adjusted without getting off the boat, but many people make fast to the dock in strange and different ways.

If there aren't any cleats available on the dock, the dock line may have to go over a piling and the eyes in most ready-made lines just aren't big enough. A surprising number of people try throwing a lasso. It may not be proper rope seamanship, but I guess it is part of our national heritage. However, a lasso can be difficult to get loose, especially if it gets wet.

There are some other solutions. Our first dock lines had eyes that were thirty inches in diameter, so the eye could fit over almost any size of piling. If you don't want to splice the big eyes yourself, several places make them up on a special order basis. We like making a big loop with a bowline, which can be made to any size and easily untied if other boats arrive later and bury your line under theirs.

Dock lines should be at least two-thirds the length of your boat and in marinas with fixed docks and big tides, long springs are a must. Those long lines create a problem that everybody encounters. After the lines are made fast, what do you do with the line that's left over? The dimensions of this problem are in direct proportion to the amount of remaining line. There are some interesting solutions.

Early in our own boating experience we flemished the extra line. On a fiberglass deck, with some dust and a little rain, it makes a very accurate print of itself. On a teak deck, a wet coil will leave a dark circle that doesn't want to go away. A boat across from us had a good bit of line flemished on the dock. Some visiting relatives stopped before going aboard and carefully wiped their feet on it.

At the other end of the scale are those who deal with leftover line in a very straightforward way. They simply throw it down in a pile. One gentleman told us that it dries out better that way. Maybe it does. Some people tidy up the extra line by wrapping it around a cleat until the thing looks like a basketball. This may solve the problem of excess line, but it's not real handy when you want to leave.

Doubling the line uses excess line to good advantage. In this case, the eye is made fast to a cleat on the boat. The line goes out around a piling and back to the boat. It can still be adjusted from the boat, uses a lot of extra line and the strength of the mooring is doubled. It's also easy to cast off when leaving the dock.

Figure 30

Figure 31
The wrong (previous page)) and right (above) methods to cleat a line.

We deal with extra line on the boat by flopping a coil of the remaining line over the rail. We use the end of the line to secure it with a couple of turns under the rail. It works well on stainless rails, but it can discolor wood rails after a while.

Securing your vessel properly makes you look good and it's safer for the boat. If you're not "tied up" at the minute, take a walk down your dock and see what remarkable solutions your neighbors have for mooring their boats and using extra dock line.

LAUNDERING LINES

We have two sets of lines. Out cruising, a 5/8 inch braided line is lighter to handle and easier on the hands. When we're going to be at dock for a while, a 3/4 inch nylon twist is a better choice. It will deal with rough weather but sunny days really beat it up. The combination of ultra violet, salt and miscellaneous grunge gradually makes the lines stiffer and harder to work with. My first mate suggested that we soak the lines in a fabric softener. That sounded like a good idea but the lines were too heavy for our washer, so we went to the local Laundromat and washed them in a heavy-duty machine.

It not only made them softer and cleaner, but they smelled better too.

MOORING & SECURING A TWIN ENGINE VESSEL

My wife and I have always handled our fifty-foot boat by ourselves. Following are some techniques we've learned, modified by experiences we've had over the last forty years. These procedures assume situations where a second person is aboard and another on the dock. In the process of any landing, the first mate will have to readjust the length of the lines. Cooperation and practice are required. The captain should stay in charge and tell the people on the dock exactly what he wants them to do. People are sometimes too helpful. We prefer to fasten the boat to cleats rather than pilings, (many of which may be eaten away below the water and are weak) but we often have no choice. The methods are basically the same.

We call our spring lines, "aft springs and forward springs." In our opinion, those names are less confusing than "after bow springs and forward quarter springs." An aft spring keeps us from moving aft and a forward spring keeps us from going forward. The primary purpose of bow and stern lines is to hold the boat to the dock. Breast lines can also be used to hold a vessel to the dock but if they're short they shouldn't be used in tidal areas. Spring lines are primarily to keep the boat from moving ahead or astern. Bow and stern lines extending forward and aft of the vessel may help to keep the boat from moving back and forth. In areas where the tidal range is great, all dock lines should be longer to allow the vessel to move vertically.

We think it makes little sense to have fenders in place before you know exactly where they should be located. Set prematurely, they may even hang up on pilings or get in the way of setting the lines. Lines should be positioned so they don't interfere with anyone getting on or off the boat. A friend of ours was a hard drinking sailor. After winning a race, there was a great celebration. He leaped off the boat, caught his foot on a spring line and rotated vigorously to the dock, breaking three ribs.

The eye of a line should be large enough to be looped over a piling or a dock cleat so lines can be adjusted without getting off the boat. Do not allow helpers on the dock to fasten the line to a cleat with knots or hitches of any kind. We are also opposed to lassos or knots that can seize up on pilings. It will create a problem getting away from the dock on a windy day if one of the lines cannot be made free.

Three things should always be done before approaching a dock:

1. Before entering a marina, be prepared for any dockage you may be directed to take, by setting out and temporarily securing at least three dock lines on each side of the vessel. The loop end of the lines should be fastened to a cleat on the boat, brought back up outside the rails and flaked down on the deck, ready to throw the eye ashore. Nothing is so lubberly as a mad scramble to find and fit dock lines just before the boat hits the dock.

2. In areas with strong currents, bring the vessel to a stop well off the dock and sit there for a minute to determine how the combination of wind and current moves your boat.

3. Center the helm. Avoid using the wheel if you can. If it isn't properly centered afterwards it may create problems in maneuvering.

Many different situations will be encountered in various locations. We will only cover the most common here.

LANDING PARALLEL TO THE DOCK

FIRST SITUATION
NO CURRENT OR WIND
AND NO OTHER VESSELS

Position the boat so you can approach the dock at approximately thirty degrees. Using the clutches only, bring the vessel in to the dock in a gradual curve so it arrives abeam at the dock. We do not throw the bow line first. We use a bow spring (fastened aft of the bow) first, which my first mate adjusts as we come closer to the dock. When it's secured, I put the engine nearest the dock in forward gear, which brings the stern in and holds it against the dock. If the bow line is used as a spring, the curve of the hull may not allow the stern to come to the dock. Without current or wind, the engine idling in forward gear will hold the boat in place, while the stern line is attached to the dock from the side of the stern away from the dock. The bow line is next. Finally, we bring one of the now unused lines over from the other side to use for an aft spring that goes forward from the aft end of the vessel.

SECOND SITUATION
WIND OR CURRENT BLOWING THE BOAT
AWAY FROM THE DOCK WITH NO OTHER VESSELS

Approach the dock at a much sharper angle, -

near sixty degrees. We allow the bow line to be taken but left with considerable slack. Use both engines (forward on inside engine, aft on outside engine) to rotate the vessel more parallel to the dock. The bow spring should be a bit longer and made fast as quickly as possible. Go forward with the inside engine locking the vessel abeam of the dock. In some situations, a touch of the outboard engine in reverse may be needed to keep the stern in place. Then a stern line can be made fast, followed by snugging up the bow line and, finally, the aft spring is set.

THIRD SITUATION
WIND OR CURRENT BLOWING TOWARD THE DOCK

In this situation, it is important to get the boat positioned directly across from the spot where you plan to dock. If the wind is not exactly at right angles to the dock, you may have to make adjustments fore or aft as the boat drifts in. The first lines to secure are the springs to keep your vessel from moving forward or astern. That will keep your neighbors happy while the bow and stern lines are attached. We did this the first time by accident. In a crowded harbor, the only space was between two sailboats. We pulled up parallel to the space and while trying to determine if there was enough space, we realized the wind was taking us in exactly where we wanted to go. As we made a perfect landing, the captain of both of the sailboats jumped off their boats with drinks and congratulations for a marvelous maneuver.

After Forty Years --- Dave Wheeler

FOURTH SITUATION
STRONG CURRENT ON THE BOW PARALLEL TO THE DOCK
NO OTHER BOATS NEARBY

Bring the vessel in parallel to the dock, passing a long bow line to the dockmaster. Do nothing else until the current takes you back almost abeam of the dock. The engines may have to be used to bring the boat around past the curve of the hull so the stern is up to the dock. Attach a stern line, an aft spring and then a forward spring. Finally, add a shorter bow line before you take off the original bow line.

Techniques for departing are similar but basically reversed. We never head out forward; it isn't healthy for swim platforms. Instead, we go forward on the bow spring to take the stern out. How far we take the stern out depends on how close other boats may be and the wind or current. At some point, a little reverse will be required to keep the bow away from the pilings and relax the spring so it can be released.

LASSOS

Lassos are not an approved nautical technique for securing your boat but there are times when it can be very handy. However, you should avoid trying to learn how to throw a lasso when you're trying to land the boat.

Practice makes perfect and it makes most sense to learn about lassos when there's no stress and you have to time get it right. The first order of business is to get the right grip on the line. Throw it so the loop goes out horizontally. If you hold it right, it will go out nicely formed into a circle that, with practice, will drop right over the piling.

The home port on one our boats was Texas. I was coming into a very long slip at Bahia Mar when I realized we needed a line on the farthest pilings. I grabbed a line, set up the loop and threw it over the pilings. The dockmaster looked at me, then at our stern and said, "Oh, OK."

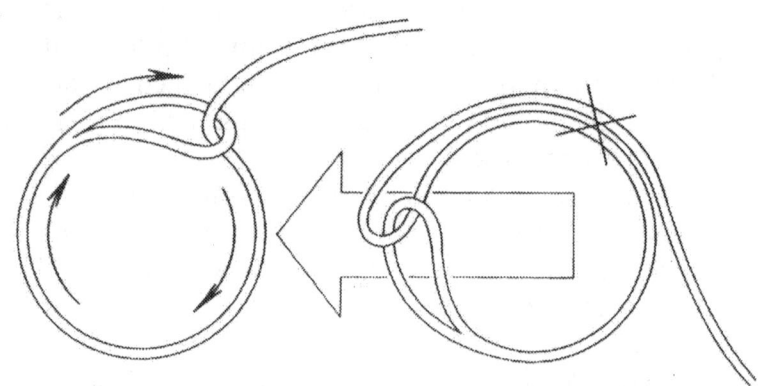

Right, the loop should be made with the standing part, or remaining line, doubled back on itself. This adds to the rotation of the loop and centrifugal force helps retain the loop size. For throwing, a loop should be held well back from the eye, about where the X is shown. Wrong, when the remaining line is not doubled back, it pulls itself through the eye as soon as it's thrown and the loop instantly gets smaller.

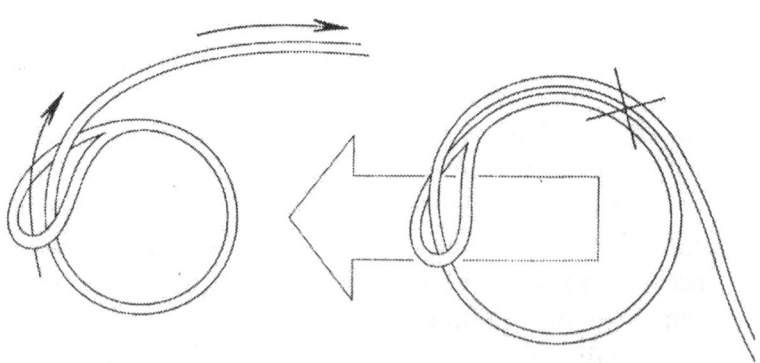

Figure 32

After Forty Years --- Dave Wheeler

BOWLINES AND CLOVE HITCHES

You don't have to be an expert with knots but there are two that will serve many purposes. A bowline (pronounced bowlin) has many uses. It can make an eye of any size right on the spot, it never jams under pressure, and because it can be easily undone, there's never a problem getting away the next morning.

These are important terms to remember. The "standing part" of the line goes back to the remaining part of the line. It just stands there while you work with the other end, which is the "working part." Any discussion of knots has to be accompanied by illustrations or photos. It will help if you check the pictures as you try these knots.

Figure 33

A bowline (pronounced bowlin) may be the most useful mariner's knot. It can make an eye of any size, it never jams under pressure and can be easily undone.

There are bowline tricks allowing you to tie it

After Forty Years --- Dave Wheeler

behind your back or with one hand but those are for marlinspike instructors or guys trying to impress their girlfriends. We'll concentrate on simple. Lines do need to be reasonably soft to make a good bowline. A pull on the standing part of a bowline tightens the knot because the loop in the standing part is constricted around the working part, making the knot stronger. The loops in an old stiff line resist being pulled together and the bowline may not be as strong.

    I think I can do this blindfolded but I may mumble something about rabbits. That was the way I first learned it and it works for me. Make a small loop in the standing part so that the line (the standing part) leading away from that loop is under the working part. The bitter end of the working part comes up through the small loop from the bottom, then around in back of the standing part and down through that loop again. The experts say that the end should wind up inside the big loop but it works either way. Keep the overall shape of the loop and the knot intact as you tighten it up.

    Now back to the memory device. Make a small loop so the working part of the line is over the standing part. That loop is the rabbit's hole. As you intone, "the rabbit comes out of his hole", you bring the end of the working part up through the loop. "Then the rabbit runs around the tree", as the working end goes around the standing part and, finally, "the rabbit jumps back in its hole", as you insert the working end back down through the loop. If that doesn't sound salty enough, you can change it to "The captain comes up from below, walks around the mast to check his ship and then goes back below." Bowlines can be used to join two lines. It's called a "bowline bend", which consists of two lines with bowlines in the end of each line, tied through each other. We used one during a storm to reach a distant piling.

    The clove hitch is probably the most misused

knot. The worst case we encountered was in a municipal marina where the young man who came out to help us simply wound the first line around a piling a couple of times and then ran back toward the stern, while the first line was coming loose. After some other bad moves, we asked him to go away and secured the boat ourselves. I asked the kid later if this was his first day and he said, "No, the city transferred me from garbage collection yesterday."

Most books say that the clove hitch is a temporary hitch and if a load is applied to only one end, the knot may slip. I'm not sure about that. A fender attached to a rail with a clove hitch appears to be very secure. Most boaters use a clove hitch (or some variant thereof) because they think it is the proper way to secure the boat.

Figure 34

Most books say that the clove hitch is a temporary hitch and if a load is applied to only one end, the knot may slip.

The line is usually put around the piling with the

working end dangling loose. As the boat moves around a bit with waves, wind, or people getting aboard the clove hitch might possibly loosen, particularly with new and slippery braided lines.

A clove hitch is made by throwing a loop over the piling. The standing part should be over the working part. Then a second loop is formed with the working part under the line coming from the first loop. If it's done correctly, the two inside lines around the piling will be parallel and next to each other. To prevent it from slipping, keep a longer working part, bring it on around the piling and tie a couple of half hitches around the standing part. That makes an ugly knot. It would be simpler and more secure to take a turn around the piling and fasten it with a pair of half hitches.

UNIVERSAL FENDERS

This requires the type of fenders that have a hole through the center. It takes two pieces of 3/8" line. On floating docks with no pilings, fenders need to be hung vertical and where there are pilings, fenders are more effective hung horizontally. We invented a system to do either one with our fenders. The first line is about ten feet long. (The best line lengths will vary with the size of your boat.) One end goes through the center of the fender and a loop is tied at the end of it. The loop will keep it from coming out and it is where the second line will be attached. Another knot has to be tied in that line against the other end of the fender so it can't slip out either way. The second line is about seven feet long with a snap hook in one end.

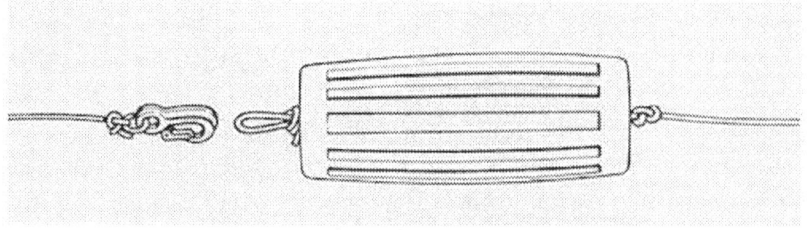

Figure 35
On floating docks without pilings, fenders need to be vertical. Where there are pilings the fenders have to be hung horizontally.

To hang the fender vertical, use one line coming out of the fender and set the bottom end of the fender almost touching the water. Most floating docks are close to the water. To hang the fenders horizontally, snap the second line into the loop at the end of the fender. Fenders are best located after the boat is positioned. Loosen the lines just a bit, push the boat away from the piling, get the fender horizontal where you want it and let the boat come back in to hold it in place. Then fasten the two lines at either end so the lines are near 30 degrees to either side, which should keep the fenders right where you want them.

PVC FENDER BOARDS

Hang two fenders vertically just as you would do with a heavy old wooden fender board. If your fenders have an opening in the center, put a loop at the bottom end of a line going through the fender. Put a stop knot just above the fender so the line won't slip out. This line will hold the fender vertically.

Put end caps on a piece of 4 inch PVC pipe about 5 feet long. The length of the pipe will vary according to the size of your boat. Drill holes all the way through the pipe, about nine inches in from the ends. The holes should be just big enough for 3/8" lines to pass through. Put a knot in the middle of each line and pass it through the holes in the PVC. Pull the line tight against the pipe and then put a knot on the other side of the pipe. To position the pipe on the fender so it won't slip off, tie the upper part of the line to the top of the fender and tie the lower part of the line to the bottom of the fender. Snaps can make it easier to attach the positioning lines to the fender.

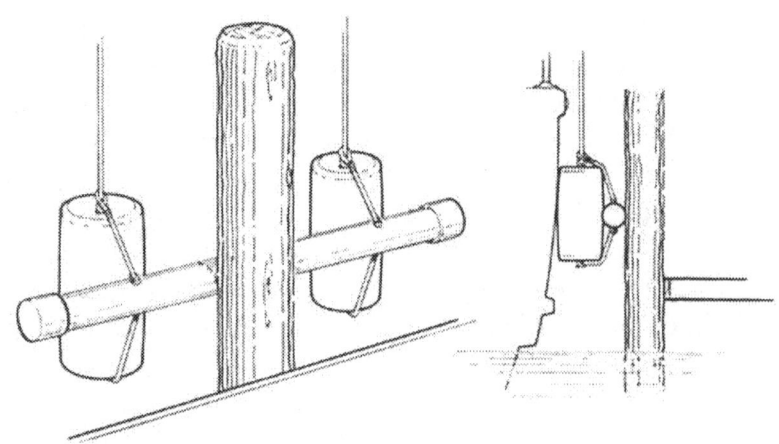

Figure 36
PVC pipe is readily available, easily replaced and its lighter weight makes it easy to set up.

The system has several advantages. PVC pipe is readily available and easy to replace. Its lighter weight makes it easier to set up. Lines fastened at the top and at the bottom of the fenders keep the pipe and the fenders in the proper relationship. PVC is slick, while the wide surface of wooden fender boards grinds against pilings, often unseating it. At the same time, the fender is rubbed against the hull, often leaving marks. These effects are reduced because the round pipe and the usually round pilings make a minimum contact point.

After Forty Years --- Dave Wheeler

Chapter Twenty-One
MOORING

MOORING BALLS

    There aren't many moorings in Florida or the Southeast but in the Bahamas moorings are everywhere. New England is about the only place we've seen moorings and, if you're not from "down East", you may be in trouble. Right up front, I should admit I'm a fresh water sailor and moorings were virtually nonexistent in the Great Lakes. Our first experience with moorings was in Nantucket with a new boat. The marina was full and they suggested we take a mooring. The resulting exercise would have made good material for a Laurel & Hardy movie.

    We didn't have enough sense to head directly into the wind as we approached the mooring, which didn't help. The bow of our new boat was seven feet above the water and I couldn't see the mooring ball at all. However,

After Forty Years --- *Dave Wheeler*

I did have a remarkable view of the first mate as she tried to reach the mooring. She hung so far over the bow that I feared for her life. I could also hear her, but her remarks were not exactly instructive, at least not about the mooring.

After that fiasco, we practiced and studied. Now we approach the mooring heading directly into the wind which provides the best control, balancing the boat's power against the wind. From a sailboat, one can reach the mooring over the bow but on our trawler, we have to run alongside of it. The first mate picks up the mooring pennant with a boat hook and walks it up to the bow. We have a "cat hole", which is the proper marine term for a large opening where lines can be brought in to a deck cleat. While I work at keeping the boat in the right place, she pulls the line up until she can pull the pennant eye through the aforementioned cat hole and put it over the cleat.

We don't want to bring chain on deck because it scratches teak decks and is usually covered with mud and slime. Sometimes the pennant is also covered with slime. To be prepared for that situation we have a line with loops in both ends. It's fastened to the cleat and the other end hangs out of the cat hole. We run our line through the loop of the pennant and back to the deck cleat.

To depart, we let go of the line we put through the pennant eye. When leaving, be careful to drift back far enough and turn to clear the mooring lines. After we learned how to work with moorings, we take them wherever possible. Securing your boat on a mooring is far easier than dealing with docking lines and fenders. It's better than anchoring because a good mooring is already securely anchored to the bottom. In heavy weather a good mooring may be the best situation of all. Of course, a generator and ample water aboard are necessary.

After Forty Years --- Dave Wheeler

ANCHORING

In theory, the type of anchor to use should be determined by wind, current and type of bottom. The lightweight anchor designed by R. S. Danforth is probably the most common anchor on pleasure craft today. It is said to be excellent in mud and sand but may not hold in grassy bottoms. The CQR plow is reputed to be effective in a wide variety of bottoms. Demonstrations of the Bruce anchor rolling over to re-imbed itself are very impressive. The Yachtsman and the Northill anchors may be the proper solution for rocky bottoms. In reality, none of that matters as much as the manufacturers think.

The fact is that very few boats make decisions about which anchor they'll put down and just use the anchor they have. Nine out of ten boats have a single anchor pulpit and one anchor. Changing anchors is not something you do on the spur of the moment and in bad weather, don't even think about it. Even if the weather was perfect and you were able to change anchors easily, you still wouldn't do it. The anchor on the pulpit is the one you put there because *it's the one you want to use.* It's there because that's the anchor *you believe in.* It's sort of a faith thing. If that anchor has held you in place in bad weather, you not only believe in it, but you're ready to take on anyone that dares to disparage it. You *need* to believe in it. On the other hand, if you dragged on a dark, stormy night, you'll never forget what was at the end of that anchor rode.

These passionate beliefs are not necessarily accurate. We have a sixty pound CQR plow anchor with 200 feet of 3/8 inch chain which is the ground tackle we believe in. It's held us fast in some heavy weather. We seldom put down a second anchor because two rodes can ruin your day if they get tangled..

Our backup anchor is a T3000 Danforth Deepset Hi-Tensile anchor. It never saw the water until the day a tropical storm was coming our way and threatening to turn worse. We finally dropped the second anchor. The storm turned away after blowing for a while and we found ourselves in a very embarrassing situation. After separating the rodes, we could not get the Danforth out of the bottom. The wind had come around and put us squarely on the Danforth which dug so far down it just wouldn't budge. We spent hours pulling every which way, doing every thing we could think of to break it loose. People came to help and when it finally came up there was a ball of clay and mud on it three feet around. We pried off all we could and then ran for miles with it dragging off the bow before all the clay came loose.

We still use only one anchor and avoid putting out a second one. However, there is a little change in the way we think. The CQR is certainly a great anchor, and with all that chain laying in a flat line along the bottom, holds very well. The Danforth is still our second anchor. However, I don't put it down unless I really have to.

HANGING OUT IN THE BAHAMAS

Many boaters have a ceremonial anchor that sits out on the bow unused, some gleaming with shiny white paint, or even chrome plated. If you're thinking about visiting the Bahamas, you will get your anchor down and dirty. Look around you. All the serious island cruisers you've admired have anchors encrusted with coral marl that looks like concrete.

There are fine marinas in the Bahamas, but you won't really experience the islands unless you spend time in the anchorages, swinging with the wind, watching your view of the harbor change and listening to the waves talk to you through the hull at night. Far away from the lights of civilization, where the night sky turns to black velvet, studded with stars, you realize how insignificant we really are..

To truly enjoy being at anchor you need ground tackle you can depend on. All the experts agree that regardless of the kind of anchor you put down, an all chain rode will lay flat on the bottom and create more horizontal pull which helps the anchor dig deeper. Scope is important and, if there's room in the harbor, an anchor line seven times as long as the distance from your bow to the bottom is most likely to keep you in place. Very few boaters put out that much rode. For one thing, there's seldom room to do it. Diving on the anchor or checking it with a glass bottom bucket is worth doing because you won't know how your anchor is positioned unless you look at it. Deep, clean, hard sand, coral marl or mud can provide good holding, but in gravel, grass or hard coral your anchor may skid along the bottom. A number of people carry the old yachtsman's anchor with hooks that can nail you fast to the bottom in rocky areas. No matter which anchor you drop or what the bottom is like, don't forget to pull the dinghy up close to the boat so the towline doesn't get wrapped around the prop as you maneuver to set the hook. We've *almost* never forgotten that.

The boat's position in the harbor has a great effect on your security and peace of mind. We can spot the guys who know what they're doing because they cruise all through the harbor, evaluating every situation and every spot before they anchor. In shallow harbors, it's also nice to have enough water under the boat to stay afloat when low tide arrives. When the anchor sets and the line is out, we walk all around the boat and visualize how our position will relate to the shore and to the other

After Forty Years --- Dave Wheeler

boats in the harbor when the wind changes. We don't hesitate to move; it's a lot better to lift the anchor and move right away than later on when there's a problem. Once we set the anchor, we turn the radar on and trace the outline of the nearest shore on the screen with a grease pencil. We can check our position with this outline, day or night. Some of the older radar were excellent for this technique because the surface screen could rotate and we could use one outline as the boat swung. On our present radar, we have to draw several outlines until we get a pattern established.

Problems occur in most anchorages. A long scope is good for holding but it creates a larger circle to swing through as the wind changes. Many sailors use two anchors as a standard procedure. They give you a smaller swinging circle and keep most of the pull on an anchor that's set in the right direction. However, the places where two anchors must be used usually have powerful currents, so you're going to turn several times. Two anchors can often be a problem when everything tangles.

Never anchor in a mooring field as moorings require less scope than anchoring. You could be sitting in your neighbor's cockpit when the wind shifts. On a very low tide, a boat nearby could be sitting on the bottom and not move with the wind at all. This may not be apparent before the boats go from adjacent to adjoining.

The "Snuggle Up Syndrome" is a common problem. This is the tendency to go where the other boats are because that must be a good place. Sometimes this deteriorates into a game of leapfrog. One boat is sitting in the harbor, when another boat arrives and goes way in beyond him. Maybe it does look like better protection in there, so after awhile the first boat moves further in. The second boat may start looking around again but the winner of this game goes hard aground.

There are "inside" and "outside" boats. Some

people like to be well inside the harbor for the best protection, but closer to land is closer to mosquitoes. Out in the open there's a better breeze and no bugs. The outside people say that if the wind comes up and they drag, they'll have time to reset the anchor before hitting the beach.

Then there's the psychological problems. Some harbors have bad reputations and the best anchors in the world aren't going to keep you from getting up at night to check your position. Noises at night get your attention in these spots and you'll need to identify all the rattles and clacks. Waves in those places always make more noise when they hit the hull. Some nights, in a remote harbor, it's inky black out there and you sure wish there was one little light someplace so you could tell if you're facing the same way. It's the law in the Bahamas that an anchor light must be shown in a designated anchorage, but there are always a few who don't. Many experienced sailors put out a lower light, often on the end of the boom. Boaters entering the harbor may be concentrating on looking around near water level and not see an anchor light at the top of a mast. A strobe light is our choice at anchor in the Bahamas.

Experts will tell you that the cost of anchoring can be drastically reduced by using cold plates, smaller generators, solar panels or wind generators. It's true, but there are serious cost/benefit considerations. These are expensive changes to make. However, if the investment is amortized over several years, you'll come out ahead. If you plan to spend a lot of time in the islands or if you plan to visit some of the more remote parts of the Bahamas, it may be the only way to go.

If you decide to do some anchoring you'll want your own water supplies. You either have to carry it, catch it, make it or fetch it. If your boat has large water tanks you can be more independent. Sailboats usually have fairly small water tanks but sailors are adept at catching rainwater. A good rain shower can add many gallons to the water supply if it's channeled to the tanks.

Water costs money in the Bahamas. It is less expensive in the Abacos than in the Exumas. The average cost of water in the Exumas this year was around fifty cents a gallon. Marsh Harbour charges less for water than Man of War, Hope Town or Guana, where they're dependent on rainfall. Some of the outer islands like Green Turtle and Spanish Cay have invested in enormous water makers. However, this doesn't make the water less expensive because they still have to prorate the cost of the equipment. Saving water saves a few cents and you don't have to put on your clothes, up anchor and go back to a marina when you run out. A watermaker is the only "all weather" solution. It will free you of dependence on rain or marinas and it's worth the cost if you plan to cruise to the islands for a few years.

Some people have stringent power and water budgets. We'd rather have the capability to spend time at anchor and be comfortable because we just enjoy being out there. Dropping the hook is always easier than bouncing off pilings trying to dock in the wind. Above all, there just isn't anything else like being in your own, self-contained world, looking out at a beautiful little Bahamian harbor.

At anchor, we have used the Man Overboard or Anchor Watch system in our electronics. In a heavy storm it will tell you if you have dragged, how far and in what direction.

After Forty Years --- Dave Wheeler

Chapter Twenty-Two
ENVIRONMENT

TIDES, CURRENTS & WILD WORDS

Sailors, scientists and philosophers have studied the tides since ancient times. The first connection between the moon and the tides was made in the first century AD. Pliny the Elder discovered the "lunitidal interval." That's a time relationship between the moon and the tides -- whether you can say it quickly or not. Pliny didn't know why they were related, just that the interval was constant. Galileo believed that the sea lagged behind as it tried to keep up with the rotation of the earth. Those were the more mundane ideas. One of the more dramatic theories was that the earth and sea was a living entity and its breathing caused the tides. Another far out hypothesis was that a great whirlpool in northern waters sucked in the water for six hours and then expelled it during the next six. No one seriously considered the notion of gravity until Newton came along. Everyone knows the falling apple story, but in reality, Newton was a very serious scientist who published his theories and findings in a remarkable dissertation, the *"Philosophiae Naturalis Principia Mathematica."* It may not make great reading but it included a precise statement of the tidal effects created by the gravitational pull of the moon.

The moon has always been special to earthlings. The word "lunatic" suggests its power over us and perfectly sane hospital workers insist there are far more violent crimes when the moon is full. Dreaded werewolves and blood sucking vampire bats were thought to come out at night under the influence of the moon. Coyotes howl, and witches fly on brooms.

Figure 37

Tides vary considerably. On the East coast they may be in the ten foot range while there are places where the only tide is caused by the winds.

After Forty Years --- *Dave Wheeler*

The power of the moon is indisputable. The moon creates the tides and makes the sea rise up and fall away. Tides are instinctively followed by sea creatures that inhabit tidal areas. The gulls know exactly when to search for exposed shellfish. Barnacles glued in place on a piling automatically close up when the falling water exposes them and then open back up to gather food when the water rises. Scientists have put various types of shellfish in their labs and have observed that even though they're in a tank, they still close and open according to the times of the tide.

Scientists have continued to study the tides and most of those studies are detailed and include complex mathematics. In the process, a tidal vocabulary was developed with some remarkable words and terms. When the moon and the sun are in line on one side of the earth, the sun reinforces the gravitational pull of the moon and makes the tides higher. This is called a *"syzygy"* (sizz-a-gee, one of my favorite words). High tides at the syzygy are called spring tides and that has nothing to do with the seasons. The word comes from a German base, "springen", meaning to spring up. Two times a month, the moon and the sun are at right angles in their relationship to earth and they are said to be in "quadrature." This causes the sun's gravity to lessen the gravitational effect of the moon and there are lower tides than usual called *"Neap tides."* The declination of the moon and sun can add to tidal effects when they happen to synchronize and cause *"Equinoctal tides."*

The basics of the tidal phenomenon are different than you might expect. Galileo was a bit closer than he thought. The tide is not highest when the moon is over that particular place. The most important force involved is horizontal since the water is more easily moved horizontally than vertically. As the earth rotates, there is a centrifugal force that might well take the water on out to space if it were not for gravity. The water does not rise straight up. The moon pulls the water horizontally and creates sort of a wave moving around the earth behind the moon. A bulge, or wave of water, is created on the side of the earth the moon has just passed. That thins out the water on the earth at right angles to the bulge. It is not shallower on the other side of the earth because the centrifugal force is still there and now it is not affected by other forces. Contributing to these effects, the wind can reinforce or diminish the wave effect. In addition the lunar orbit around earth is not concentric and its distance from the earth changes. Obviously, when it is closer it has more effect.

A *seiche* is an interesting phenomenon although not exactly a tide. They're more common in the Great Lakes, created by strong and steady winds from one direction. The water is moved toward one end of a lake and the surface is essentially tilted, higher at the leeward end and much lower at the windward end, where the wind is coming from. We have not experienced a major seiche, but at the Toledo Yacht Club,on Lake Erie, a powerful seiche removed *all the water* from their harbor. Yachts were lying on the bottom with bent shafts and twisted propellers. At the end of one dock was a huge pile of old beer cans.

The power and speed of currents are directly proportional to the tidal range. The more the tide goes up and down, the stronger the current going in and out. Current cleans the water. Miami, even with its population density, still has clear water because of strong currents and open access to ocean waters. The water in Nassau is surprisingly clear and again there is powerful current and the harbor is open to great depths at either end.

At anchor, the current in some places in the Exumas is very powerful and a boat at anchor does strange things. You expect the wind to be coming over the bow but the strong currents take precedence and the bow points into the current while the wind blows in from the side or even from the rear of the boat. The current forces you to put out two anchors and after a few hassles with tangled anchor lines, you get very conscious of the current.

Exuma Sound drops off to over three hundred fathoms almost immediately after leaving one of the cuts. The difference in depths between the sound and the bank sets up major characteristics of cruising in the Exumas. The great change in depth creates powerful currents and passing through the cuts can be exciting at least. In the enormous depths, sometimes inhabited by whales and submarines, powerful masses of water run up against a wall of rapidly decreasing depths and the water is literally pushed upwards. This mass of water is forced through the cuts in a venturi effect that can be someplace between impressive and appalling. Never try the cuts when current and wind are in opposition, or when the wind is unusually strong and coming directly in the cut. In the islands, the extremes of this situation are called a "rage."

We lived in Beaufort, South Carolina for almost a year, where tidal range is significant and resulting currents very strong. At first we thought that barnacles or shells couldn't grow on the boat in all that current. That was wrong! The current feeds the little critters and they thrive.

There has always been speculation about the evident power of the tides. It might be a nonpolluting and unending source of power for mankind. Think of the awesome power involved in the weight of water that can be moved in a high tide, forty feet of water in the Bay of Fundy, or thirty feet of water in Cook Inlet, Alaska. The power schemes revolve around the idea of capturing the water at high tide by allowing it to come through a dam and then closing the dam. The water would then be directed to some type of water wheel that generates power. The beauty of the system is that it requires no fuel, minimum maintenance and has no ill effect on the environment. Even though fuel prices continue to rise, that same inflation increases the construction costs. There have been many proposals and some have been built. France has a large and very successful installation, but the United States has done no more than study the possibilities.

There are still many extraordinary words we haven't even mentioned, like diurnal inequality, amphidromes, synodical months and proxigean springs, but perhaps we should look at "Tsunami." The general public calls them "tidal waves". In Japanese it means big wave in the harbor, which is accurate, because these waves are awesome only when they reach shallow water. Almost all of the Tsunamis occur in the Pacific, usually associated with earthquakes or volcanic eruptions at the bottom of the sea. There have been over 50 in Japan as well others in Hawaii, New Zealand, Philippines and Alaska. Probably the most famous was the 1883 volcano eruption in Krakatoa. It started with several violent explosions and then the entire island blew up, leaving a crater 5 miles wide and 800 feet deep. The noise was heard 3000 miles away. It created a Tsunami 120 feet high, which became a wall of water, destroying hundreds of towns and villages and killing 37,000 people.

Scientists say that, theoretically, a Tsunami wave could reach heights of 250 feet. An earthquake underwater can push water away at 500 miles an hour. It becomes a fantastic current within the body of water with very little evidence of the phenomena at the surface. Naval ships, passed by a Tsunami wave, have reported seeing waves only two feet high. When this mass of water, moving at incredible speed, hits the shallows, it essentially does a somersault. The water at the bottom of this mass is held back by the bottom, tripping its toes. A basic law of hydraulics is that water is not compressible. As a result, the mass of water retains its size and rises up over the bottom. The upward movement creates the enormous waves as it comes up over the shallows--a very big wave in the harbor. The water continues to roll forward, usually creating eight great waves. If the cove, bight or harbor has a funnel shaped entrance, a venturi effect is created which increases its speed and dramatically increases the size of the waves. I assume it would be possible to have a tsunami, a syzygy, an extreme spring tide and a hurricane at the same time. I don't know what you'd call it, but the results are surely unpronounceable and unimaginable.

OCEAN CURRENTS OF THE WORLD

We are all participants in the planet's systems at a variety of levels. We started with a little sailboat. We went through many ridiculous, and sometimes embarrassing, efforts before we learned to make the boat do what we wanted. It was quite a while and several boats later before we began to appreciate the environment we were working in. We learned to use winds, tides and currents to better advantage and learned more about the weather. Observing your surroundings, such as which way birds on pilings are facing or the direction leaves in the water are moving, provides useful information. Learn to cooperate with these forces and use them to your advantage.

At a greater level, the currents of the oceans are much more than a force that can help propel your boat. Most serious cruisers are aware of the great currents of the oceans and how they may be used or dealt with but using them as a cruising tool may be an introverted view..

The earliest travelers on earth were sailors and, eventually, the great sailing ships explored the farthest points of the planet searching for whales. Europeans had well developed cultures long before they considered exploring North America. The Spaniards followed the currents and were the first to establish themselves in the Carribean. Later, the Gulf Stream led them along the eastern shores of North America; as a result they dominated Florida and the entire east coast of the continent at one time. Currents in the northern reaches of the Atlantic delineate the early travels of the Vikings.

As a result of our space programs, we know much more about ocean currents. The TOPEX/Poseidon mission developed charts of the oceans currents. Gyres are a system of ocean currents rotating clockwise in the northern hemisphere and counterclockwise in the southern hemisphere. The mission confirmed that the strongest currents are not at the edges of the gyres but near the centers. It also showed that counter currents were sometimes created at the edges of major currents. Many countries have released hundreds of drifter buoys that measure temperature, salinity, barometric pressure and the direction and speed of ocean currents.

At one time, the most common device for measuring currents was a container with a compass and a propeller. Its location was recorded and, in addition to the direction of the device, the speed at which the propeller rotated provided the current's speed. Oceanographers express current flow in "millions of cubic meters per second." The Gulf Stream current flow is 150 million cubic meters per second, as opposed to the average of 10 to 20 million cubic meters per second for deep water western boundary currents. Today moored, computerized buoys provide much of that information. Drifting buoys also provide position, water temperature and salinity. These currents influence climates and establish routes for explorers and oceangoing ships.

As currents flow along a coastline, they encounter resistance from land masses. This tears off a piece of the current which becomes a whirlpool or an eddy. As the Gulf Stream flows north, it encounters cold water coming south. As the currents conflict, portions of both currents are torn away and become independently rotating systems, known as rings. These rings may cover a considerable distance while retaining their characteristics. The colder rings result in plankton rich water that feeds many pelagic creatures.

WEATHER

Bad weather causes more offshore emergencies than anything else. Make sure you get the best weather information possible. Do not be pressured by an increasing marina bill, people who think you're cowardly or guys on the dock who claim they can handle rough weather. There is no vessel impervious to bad weather. Don't ignore the simple, standard sources of weather information. Some AM and FM radio stations have good marine weather forecasts. Television is a good source of weather information because it shows pictures of both present and forecast weather. The problem is finding a station with weather for the area you're going to.

VHF is the standard marine radio with several weather options. It is a source the Coast Guard prefers because they have systems in place to locate you by the VHF signal. Sometimes the signal is poor because the station is too far away or there is some interference. VHF broadcast from the United States is difficult, or impossible, to hear in the Bahamas. However, there are some excellent Cruiser's Nets that relay VHF broadcasts from the United States to the Bahamas and the Caribbean.

SINGLE SIDE BAND (SSB)

Audio signals made by your voice are impressed on a radio signal by modulation. The two most common types are AM (amplitude modulation) and FM (frequency modulation.) A base signal, called the carrier, is continuously broadcast in an AM modulated radio signal. Above and below this base signal is a sideband. These are modulated, or varied in some way. The sound you hear on an AM broadcast is from the two sidebands.

The first marine radios used the sidebands without the carrier. Those were the DSB or double sideband radios, long ago replaced by VHF (very high frequency) radios. VHF has a shorter range and limits the range of interference. The old DSB radios created interference at great distances. Single sideband radio transmissions can use either the lower or the upper sideband. Using a single sideband is much more efficient because all of the radio's power is channeled into one sideband. This is why SSB radios are an excellent choice for long distance transmissions. SSB radios normally have 150 watts of power but amplifiers can increase their power.

There isn't room here for a great deal of detailed technical information, but if you buy a good SSB radio, the manuals will not only cover the operation but much of the theory and technical data as well. "Propagation" is one thing that you need to know about. It's a factor you will sometimes curse and sometimes marvel at. There are two prime ways that radio waves travel through the air. Stations broadcasting on lower frequencies, or within a hundred miles or so, reach you by very dependable "ground waves." The SSB radios send signals that travel toward the sky and bounce back from the ionosphere. This allows great distances to be covered but this "bounce" effect can make the signal skip right over a nearby station. (We can sometimes hear California from Miami when we can't hear Jacksonville.) Propagation can be different from day to night and from season to season, but sunspots or solar storms create the most dramatic effects.

Natural noises, such as thunderstorms, can create interference. People create interference with many kinds of electrical equipment. One of the most common is fluorescent lights that create a buzz across high frequency radio. Some radio operators simply talk too much and create conflicts on many frequencies. As in every endeavor, there are nutcases -- people who purposely create interference or harass others.

A good antenna is almost as important as the radio itself. The length of an antenna must be designed for the frequency range in which the radio will be transmitting. Since different frequencies are used and it isn't possible to change the length of the antenna, a coupler can artificially change it. It's a necessary piece of equipment for a SSB radio.

The high frequency maritime service was developed for commercial vessels to communicate in the 50 to 4000 mile range, on radio frequencies from 1.8 MHz to 30 Mhz. Perhaps you will remember Walter Winchell starting his radio program with, "Good Evening, Mr. & Mrs. America and all the ships at sea." That referred to Single Side Band. They are still the prime users. Ships larger than 1600 tons are required to have a radio officer and monitor emergencies on 2.182

kHz and 500 kHz (Morse code) 15 minutes before and after each hour, at a minimum. These multi-lingual vessels have powerful radios and the power to dominate the airways. Most of those commercial stations are there for the sole purpose of conducting business.

Single Sideband has some important safety features. The Coast Guard universally monitors 2.182 MHz, twenty four hours a day for emergency traffic and several stations now provide weather information around the clock. Single sideband radios can also transmit GMDSS, which is the Global Maritime Distress Signaling System. If the radio is connected to a GPS receiver, this new feature can instantly broadcast a distress signal and your exact location with the push of a single button. All SSB radios must be type approved, which includes being designed for a marine environment.

The first Single Side Band radios were limited to a small number of approved channels. Today, there are SSB radios that can be tuned to almost a thousand preprogrammed frequencies. Although operators cannot transmit on many of these frequencies, they can listen to many different sources of information such as time standards, weather stations or amateur radio nets. The great number of frequencies available makes a large memory system very important for effective use. Almost all of these radios have a method of channel scanning, allowing you to select a number of channels that you can constantly monitor.

To operate a marine SSB transceiver on a pleasure craft, the station license for your VHF should be modified to add marine SSB, by adding "1600 kHz to 27,500 kHz to the list of frequencies requested. The vessel must also have a licensed VHF transceiver installed, the same operator's permit is required and the High Frequency transmitter must be a legal one. It must be "type approved." That is, designed in accordance

After Forty Years --- Dave Wheeler

with federal operational and technical specifications.

SSB has channels for ship to shore telephone service and presently these stations broadcast weather forecasts. The future of these services will be decided by the federal budget.

AMATEUR RADIO

The Waterway Radio & Cruising Club is commonly called the "Waterway Net". It's main purpose is to provide fellow amateurs on boats with safety information, communications and weather.

Clearly, its updates on conditions make it an unparalleled safety aid for cruising vessels. Licensed hams, visiting from numerous other countries, participate and many others, hams or not, listen for information about navigable waters or the latest news on hurricanes or severe weather. Membership is open to anyone holding a valid amateur radio license of any class. However, you must have a General Class license to transmit on the net.

Last April, the FCC requirements were changed and the types of license reduced from five to three. In ascending order they are Technician, General and Advanced Extra, with written tests for each. You are required to know the rules regarding how and where you can transmit, but knowing a great deal about radio technology is not obligatory. The Morse code requirement is now only five words per minute for all licenses.

The Waterway Net is one of the most successful nets in the world. It has accomplished that by operating as a controlled net. Much of that discipline is the result of rather stringent requirements by the FCC. It operates on the 40-meter band on a frequency of 7.268 kHz. Air time

After Forty Years --- Dave Wheeler

daily is 0745 to approximately 0845 Eastern Standard time.

Before the daily routine begins, specific members have been assigned to be Net Control, North Relay, South Relay and Weather Reporters. The net starts with the call, "CQ, CQ, Is the frequency clear?" (CQ means, "calling all stations" and this call is an FCC requirement.) The first order of business is a request for Emergency and Priority traffic. Emergency calls are related to the immediate safety of life or protection of a vessel. We have heard some very dramatic moments in this portion of the Net. Priority traffic is for messages of obvious urgency such as a death or the severe illness of a family member. It often includes assistance to the Coast Guard in locating overdue or missing boats.

Weather information is next. It starts with the Bahamas weather, and in storm season, the tropical weather is next. When there is a hurricane threatening the Net often works with the National Hurricane Center to help track the storms. Caribbean weather is next, then the Southwest North Atlantic weather, followed by the Gulf of Mexico and the Florida Coastal forecasts. Weather reporters will sometimes cover a special area on request, but do not make forecasts. Information from the National Weather Services is relayed, so it can be heard by mariners in distant areas.

General Announcements cover things like bridge closings, the hapless discovery of a high spot in the waterway, lost dinghies and luncheons scheduled in various places for Amateur Radio Operators. This is followed by General Traffic. The first part is for vessels actually underway, then the traffic is open to everyone. Amateurs check into the Net by responding to Net Control's request for traffic with the suffix of their call sign. For example, my call sign is NØLSK and I would use only the LSK to check in. If the reception is less than

After Forty Years --- Dave Wheeler

optimum, Net Control prefers call signs to be given in phonetics, that is, Lima Sierra Kilo.

Position Reports and Float Plans are next. Position reports are used to let friends and family members know where you are and how your cruise is progressing. Float plans are a more serious matter. They are reserved for open water or hazardous crossings. You should establish a contact person. If you file a float plan, it is your responsibility to check in every morning while that float plan is open. If you do not check in, the contact person will be notified and they will determine if the Coast Guard should be notified. If the Net cannot get in touch with you or your contact, they will notify the Coast Guard. Be advised that the Coast Guard will not be pleased if you simply forgot to call.

All this may sound a bit formal but there's another side to the Net that is almost as important. Friendships are formed, sometimes with people you've never seen. As a result, luncheons take place in a variety of locations and at least one annual party is organized where you can see what "N4WHO" actually looks like. The Waterway Radio and Cruising Club is a network of people that reaches from Canada, down the East Coast to Bermuda and the Bahamas, and as far south as Guatemala. If you need local information, help locating an engine part, or just someone to have a drink with, they're there.

There are several auxiliary nets associated with the Waterway Radio and Cruising Club. The Bahamas Weather Net is a separate group that convenes before the Net and provides additional Bahamian weather in extended areas. The Computer Net has become very popular and meets every Friday after the regular Net. The CW Net encourages the use of Morse code and offers assistance to beginners. The RV Net caters to WRCC members who also travel in Recreational Vehicles. They meet every Wednesday following the regular Net. The Tech Net was the first of the WRCC auxiliary nets. It was established to help new Amateurs with their radios, radio equipment and antennas. In fact, they helped me design our 40 meter antenna. That group meets every Sunday morning following the regular Net.

You have friends and help, no matter where you may cruise. Seventy-knot winds hit us one night and, while the anchor held, the inflatable flipped upside down, immersing the motor in salt water. Next morning on the net, I asked if anyone knew where we could take the motor to get it repaired. Fifteen minutes later, three people came aboard and put the motor back in running condition. . Now that's a safety net!

LEARNING ABOUT LIGHTNING

One morning, a light rain suddenly turned to a downpour. The wind came up and it began to thunder as we rushed below to batten down the portholes. The lightning was slashing down and suddenly there was a blinding flash of light and a tremendous blast of sound-- like an artillery gun going off. No z-z-z-t, no nothing, just WHAM! We peered out of the portholes and said, "Wow, something close got hit with that one." It never crossed our mind that it could have been us. We've been cruising the east coast for 30 years and getting hit with lightning seemed to be as likely as winning the lottery. The boat wasn't out in open water but "safely moored" at the dock in our marina. When we went above to look around, we found the console in the pilothouse of our trawler was blown loose and some of the instruments were on the floor.

After Forty Years --- Dave Wheeler

Figure 38

Lightning had hit the aluminum pipe masts that supported our amateur radio antenna. The antenna wire was gone, the top of the aft mast was pulverized and there was nothing left of the light on the forward mast but a black blob. The wires inside the mast were fried, and on top of the pilothouse, the lightning had arced across the cables between our satellite dish and the GPS antenna. Down below, the satellite receiver showed no signs of life and the VCR connected to it didn't work. The television worked but had a slightly purple area in the middle of the picture. Fortunately, we didn't rush out and buy a new TV as the purple cleared up after a few days.

We could smell smoke or burnt plastic and in the engine room found that the alternator windings on the starboard engine had been melted together. The engines seemed to be okay, but the boat had to be taken for a trial run after things were back together. The meter on the front of the battery charger was blown out and the plastic cover was on the other side of the engine room.

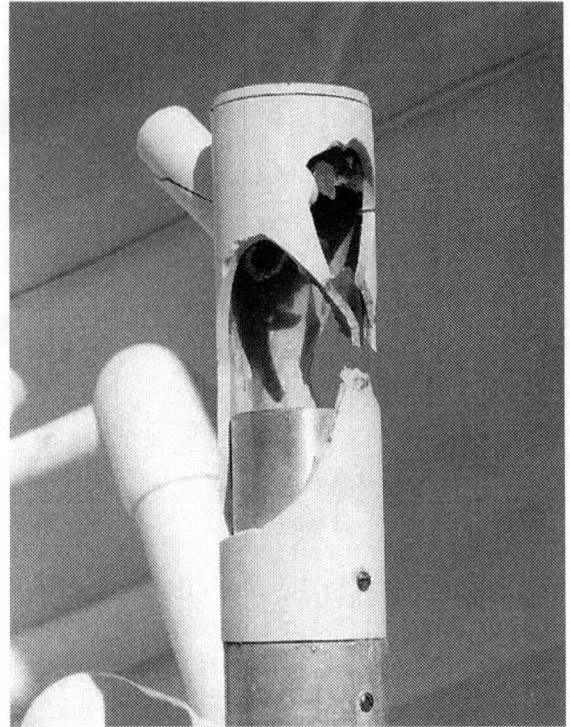

Figure 39
Lighting can cause major damage and even sink vessels.

We have a small bilge pump that comes on automatically every five minutes or so and we soon realized that it wasn't working. If water gets above a certain level in the boat, a larger pump comes on with an alarm. Fortunately, it's never done that except when tested. When we lifted the hatches, we found the switch to the big bilge pump wasn't working either. It was obviously time to take a serious look all through the boat. Our first concern was the hull. Boats have had holes blown in the bottom by lightning strikes but ours seemed to be OK. The bilge pumps were put back in operation and all the through hull fittings seemed sound, although the pumps were running a bit more than usual. It took two days before we tracked down a pinhole in one of the through hull fittings. It appeared to be the result of corrosion and not related to the lightning strike.

We had a ground plate with a massive switch that was designed to deflect lightning from the ham radio gear to the ground plate. It worked for the amplifier but the radio was dead, probably because it was a more sensitive piece of equipment. Forward, part of the strike on the higher mast came down through the stays near the twelve volt deck lights. A charred line went from the each of the bolts holding the stays to the nearby 12V deck lights, which was where current moved into the 12V system.

Inside the pilothouse console, there was apparently an explosive force as well as an electrical force. There was no evidence of burning or charring when we first looked inside. One of the experts I talked to said the strike created the explosion as it vaporized the moisture in the air inside the console. We lost our AM/FM stereo radio, the ICOM VHF radio, our backup VHF radio and a two meter radio base station. The depth finder and the log were not functioning and we thought it odd that while the radar was on and stayed on after the lightning hit, the chart plotter that operates through it was dead. The radar looked fine when we turned it on, but a couple of days later someone pointed out that the picture didn't change and one segment was missing. After the obvious results of the strike, we began to see the most insidious effects of lightning -- the unseen, hidden damage that often becomes evident much later.

By now we were reeling, afraid the damage might be more than we could handle. We asked three local companies to come in and check everything out. The compass bowl had a crack in it. One of the pieces from the console may have hit it or it was weakened by sun and the physical jar from the strike cracked it. The center windshield wiper wasn't working at all. It turned out that the wiper motor was OK but the control in the instrument panel had a wire that looked like a frayed rope end. The synchronizer was dead and part of it down in the engine room had that, now familiar, charred look. Several little ruby indicator lights had, literally, exploded. It must have been the design of the lights, since they were in different places, on the instrument panel, in the electric panel and in the galley. Our refrigerator was operated by 110V and 12V with an inverter. The strike came into it through the 12V system and put it completely out of business. We lived out of a cooler for a few days until some friends loaned us a small refrigerator.

As we dug further, we discovered new problems. It became evident that every device and every place that could have been damaged had to be examined. That entailed opening up each area, for example, unloading and removing all the shelves in a cabinet to check through hull fittings, unscrewing the faces of the console, clearing out a closet to check something under the bottom, or removing carpet to get into hatches that are seldom used. Time after time, I opened a cabinet or a locker and, after cleaning all the junk out, found other problems to deal with--unrelated things like a kink in a hose, or a wire with questionable insulation.

Many repairs and replacements turned out to be more complicated than expected. One tachometer on the instrument panel was pegged at 3500 rpm and never moved again. Marine Mobile Services in Key Largo, did an amazing amount of research and finally found an instrument in Texas that matched the other one. Motorola doesn't make that model any more and this was apparently the only one left in the world. When it arrived, the lettering was different and the bezel was a different color. Obviously, we had to find two matching tachometers to make the panel look right. As we worked around this problem, I realized that my other instruments had gotten a little corroded and the panel itself was pretty beat up. So, at a time when I didn't need any extra work to take up my time, I took out the panel and refinished it as well as cleaning up all the instruments.

Down below, the amateur radio gear had to come out of the cabinet so it could be properly checked, which meant undoing all the wiring. There goes at least another day.

To file the insurance claim, I put together a list of everything that was damaged, the model, whether it was still in production and what would be an appropriate replacement. It's important to know whether the insurance pays for replacement, the cost of the original equipment, or the amount you stated on the annual insurance renewal when you were threatened by higher premiums. Making that list is a major project, but if you do keep an equipment list, it's easier to bring it up to date. If you don't, start it now. The paperwork involved in a lightning strike is surprising, almost like income tax. You go over and over it, wondering if you forgot something. Then, when you have it all up to date, you find something new. A friend who's boat had been hit by lighting, said he was still finding things wrong over a year later. I found that a little frightening, but when I asked the adjuster about it, he said sometimes that does happen and they would work with me on future problems. Electronic equipment might be repaired and be completely dependable, but lightning can do some things inside tiny circuits that are not discernible.

Some flush mounted equipment that cannot be repaired may have to be replaced by a new model. If the dimensions are different, the replacement may not fit in the same hole. It's easy to enlarge a hole but making one smaller is a bit more difficult. Console or instrument panels may have to be redesigned to accommodate the

After Forty Years --- Dave Wheeler

new equipment. Much of the equipment on my boat was put together over a long period of time. I researched each item, decided where I wanted it, and because I was only doing one project at a time, I could spend many hours on each installation. Now I was faced with dozens of problems that all demanded attention right away. I certainly didn't want to do all this again if there was any way to prevent it. Therefore, I started digging around to find out more about lightning and if there was any reasonable way to reduce the chances of getting zapped again.

Up until now, we were convinced that we didn't need lightning protection. We were certain that very few boats actually get hit by lightning. Besides, we thought, lightning is so powerful, that any device you put up is like building a thread fence to keep out gorillas. Now that we've become motivated to learn more, we can't believe we were that unaware of the facts. Statistics based on the percentage of all BOAT/US marine insurance claims for lightning strikes over a five year period show, the odds we were working against.

Auxiliary Sail	6 hits out of 1,000 boats
Multihull Sail	5 hits out of 1,000 boats
Trawlers	3 hits out of 1,000 boats
Sail only	2 hits out of 1,000 boats
Cruisers	1 hit out of 1,000 boats
Runabouts	2 hits out of 10,000 boats

An article in the Professional Boatbuilder Magazine, said that 1 in every 15 yachtsmen will experience a lightning strike, 1 in every 9 boats will suffer damage and 8 out of 10 cruising sailboats will be struck at least once in its lifetime.

Let's get real. There are 100 lightning strikes every second, somewhere on this planet. 1,600,000

After Forty Years --- Dave Wheeler

strikes come down from cloud to ground. Hundreds of people are killed by lightning every year and there you are, out on the water sailing around, creating a lonely and a very attractive target.

Lightning is static electricity multiplied many times. When we were kids, we used to scuff our feet on carpets and then touch fingers to see the big spark. As cold air in a storm cloud falls and warm air rises, the air masses rub against each other and create an electric charge, usually positive at the top of the cloud and negative at the bottom. These opposite charges seek to eliminate the difference and do so by creating an enormous spark called lightning. This difference is called potential. A larger difference equals a greater potential that it seeks to equalize. Most lightning or equalization occurs within the cloud but when the potential is very great, it reaches out to other clouds or to the earth.

When the intensity of a thunderstorm increases, an internal negative charge increases in the cloud and a positive charge is generated on the earth's surface below it. As the storm moves, the earth's positive charge follows it like a magnetized shadow. That positive charge on the earth's surface becomes more concentrated at any point that is higher than the surrounding area. The magnetic attraction of the opposite polarity literally pulls the ground charge up into the highest point. Picture a zillion little plus signs spread out over the water that are now jammed into the top of a church steeple, a radio tower or even a boat. This also creates the "zone of protection" because those plus signs, or electrons, rushing up to the highest point have reduced the number of positive electrons in the area immediately below it.

When the potential or imbalance becomes great enough, it can overcome the insulating or dielectric qualities of the air and *WHAM!* An equalizing arc occurs. That arc of lightning can be powerful enough to supply lights for a small city. The temperature at the core of a strike is five times hotter than the surface of the sun and an instant delivery of 25,000 amps can be catastrophic. We've all seen pictures of a splintered tree -- think mast. There are two types of strikes. Most are cloud negative to ground positive, but there is usually one strike in each storm that brings down a positive charge. These are about five times as strong and disastrous. There are also secondary effects that can be dangerous. There can be side flashes as well as electromagnetic pulses that are particularly deadly for electronic gear.

Cloud to ground lightning is actually a series of events. The arc starts as a leader that branches out, forming the forked appearance. Each branch is about 150 feet long but none of these reach the earth's surface. An opposite charged object sends up a streamer to meet it, which provides an ionized path for the lightning.

There are several things that can be done. Direct the strike away from the boat, make the boat less attractive to lightning, or minimize the damage if you do get hit. A lightning rod is the traditional approach, an element taller than any surrounding structures that can direct the energy of the strike to a ground point where it will do no harm. On a sailboat, a wire from the top of the mast straight down to salt water might work. A powerboat can not usually bring a straight line down outside because the angle is too great. Lightning goes anywhere it wants to and that's a direct path to ground. Direct means straight, lightning doesn't like turns. If it can't find a straight path, it gets frustrated and destroys anything that gets in its way. A sailboat with a metal mast going straight down through the main cabin to a metallic keel would create the best path, but the architecture of many boats (and most powerboats) makes it difficult to establish that straight path to ground. That

After Forty Years --- Dave Wheeler

direct path does make a difference. A friend's sailboat had a mast stepped on the trunk cabin top with no attachment to ground. After the boat was hit by lightning, the interior looked like an insane thing had tried to get out of it. Burned spots, unrelated areas of destruction and small charred holes were all over the inside of the boat.

Static dissipaters are those fuzzy things some people have on their mast tops. The intent is to reduce the buildup of the ground charge so it will not reach the point of creating a streamer. These devices look like feather dusters or bottle brushes made of wire, creating a mass of points. Ground charges become concentrated in the smallest and highest points. Because there isn't enough room in these tiny wires to contain all of those little plus signs or positive electrons that want to get in there, some are lost to the atmosphere, or dissipated. This reduces the electrical potential of your boat and makes it less attractive to a strike. However, because it is the highest point on your vessel, you should still provide as direct a path to ground as possible.

The Lightning Master Corporation in Clearwater, Florida makes the "fuzzy ball" you've seen on many sailboat masts. They also design and manufacture systems to protect airports, cellular phone towers and broadcasting stations. Lightning Master is distributed by Forespar Marine of Rancho Santa Margarita, California.

The third approach is to minimize the power and the effects of a strike. The first order of business is a clear path to ground. If this doesn't exist, lightning will seek any path such as miscellaneous wires, stays, even halyards, and when that path is not a good conductor, heat is created. The frantic need for a clear path to ground makes lightning crazy and it will take that search into strange and unexpected places. You can't control it. The best you can do is guide it. A large square ground plate, connected as directly as possible to the highest point on your boat, can discharge some of that power and keep it away from more vulnerable things.

The ABYC suggests that all metallic and electrical masses of a boat should be electrically bonded together to provide a low resistance path to equalize potential in a strike. One prime reason for bonding is to avoid having a human body create a path for the current in a strike. Secondary or side effects can be reduced or prevented by bonding. One such effect is a side flash. The straight through flow of lightning current from strike point to ground may leave some areas out of that direct path with a residual imbalance. This potential will send current to the area of impact to equalize it. Side flashes can be just as deadly as the original hit because people think it's all over and they make contact with something that still has a powerful charge. Bonding equalizes the potential between all areas that might retain a charge.

Another secondary consequence is the surge of electromagnetic energy (EMP), which may induce current in totally isolated devices. The on-off action of a lightning strike causes the electromagnetic field surrounding the strike to expand and collapse. This motion induces currents that can damage solid state electronics. EMP tends to flow on the outside of things. If the case of an instrument is grounded and has a clear path to ground, it will guide the current around the sensitive innards of your electronics.

We had surge protectors on our TV, the computer and the microwave, as well as on the telephone line coming into the boat. In some areas, when the power goes off, it comes back on line with a surge that can create damage. Equipment on our boat that was connected through surge protectors appeared to have had some protection. However, the experts tell us a lightning strike is far beyond the capabilities of most surge protectors. For normal surge protection, Radio Shack has some models with a guarantee covering damage to equipment connected with their surge protector, but it doesn't include lightning. There are more expensive units capable of dealing with lightning. Lightning Master Corporation in Clearwater, Florida, has lightning class "Transient Voltage Surge Suppressors" available. Incidentally, the basic component in a surge protector is a metal oxide varister, which will wear out and need to be replaced occasionally.

This material is the result of my own investigation and research. Many people have helped me with this article. I dare not try to list them all because it would take another page and I'd probably forget someone. There is an excellent book on the subject. "Lightning and Boats" by Michael V. Huck, Jr. Since the strike, I've read many papers, articles and books about this phenomena and I still don't understand everything about lightning. It appears I'm not alone. The power of lightning is awesome and everything I've read, no matter how expert the author, always includes a disclaimer. This is mine.

I am sure of a couple of things. Although it may take awhile to get this ship together again, we'll have a better boat because I had to dig into every corner and check everything on it. This time, we were neither hurt nor holed, but I did get the message. There are no guarantees, but I'm going to do everything I can to protect this boat and this crew.

SURVIVING STORMS

Our first big storm was Hurricane David. We rode out 85 mph winds in the center of a large slip in Spooner's Creek, an entirely enclosed marina in North Carolina. It was just the edge of the storm but we left with the mistaken idea that we could probably deal with tropical storms.

Hurricane Andrew brought reality. The officially recorded winds at the center of the hurricane were 145 mph, with gusts over 175 mph. Many observers believe the winds were well over 200 mph because 175 mph is the maximum that their instruments could read. The storm also spawned many tornadoes that could generate that level of wind speed. Outside the center, the winds were much lower. Power and telephones in Islamorada, in the Keys, went out but our boat had a generator and a ham radio. We had no idea how bad the storm had been in Homestead until we saw a Miami newspaper. A few days later, we went up to see for ourselves and were shocked by the devastation. It looked as though someone had taken an enormous rotary mower and reduced the entire area to rubble. It was apparent that Andrew could have picked up our 50 foot trawler, snapped the 3/4 inch lines like thread and thrown us far up on shore.

The only realistic solution to deal with an approaching hurricane is -- GET AWAY FROM IT! If you can't get out, or you insist on staying, these are some of the things you can do:

1. Long before the storm season, search for secure places with good holding where you can put out multiple anchors.

2. Find a big slip with good docks and solid pilings in a well-protected harbor and prepare to secure your boat in the middle of slip. The center of a canal where you can tie to trees, mangroves or anything substantial on either shore is the same basic arrangement.

3. Prepare the boat as well as you can and think again about getting out.

Figure 40
Remnants of Hurricane Andrew.

There may be variations and combinations of these elements, but you have to evaluate the storm and the conditions in your location and decide on the best approach for you and your vessel.

During storm season, we plot every named storm each day until it dies or goes away. There are computer programs that can do this for you but plotting them has become a ritual for us. The coordinates of the storm are available on the weather channels of your VHF radio and on Amateur (Ham) Radio or Single Sideband. The Waterway Net has complete weather information and when a hurricane threatens, the Net helps the National Hurricane Center track the storm. You can gather useful information by listening to the reports that hams send in from various areas, here and in the islands. If you have a computer with a modem on board, NOAA provides extensive weather coverage on the Internet. If you gather enough information about the path and the strength of the storm, you can make the best decision.

If you decide to ride it out at anchor, you will

need plenty of space, good holding and several anchors. Consider more than one place when you look around. It could be crowded when you get to that first spot and another boat coming down on you in a storm can cause serious damage. A strong, well secured mooring may be the best of all situations. Moorings are more common in the Northeast, and in the Bahamas, many people have a "storm mooring." There are few moorings in the southeast and environmental concerns prevent the installation of new ones.

Prepare for a storm surge. On a mooring or at anchor, you'll rise and fall with the flow but at a dock you can be damaged by the very things securing your boat. Key Biscayne has had surges of sixteen feet and in the northwest Bahamas, one surge was twenty three feet. It might be possible to survive a surge of that magnitude on a rock solid mooring with a great deal of scope and a lot of room but it would be a wild ride. Historically, storm surges have killed 9 out of 10 hurricane victims. In coastal areas, enormous surges can be generated by water being driven up over the continental shelf and then combined with a rising tide and waves created by the wind.

During the storm season, we live with a hurricane checklist. It reminds us what to do at the beginning of the season, what to do when a storm threatens and what must be done if we have to leave the boat.

We met Hurricane Erin in the Abacos. This time we were more experienced, better prepared and had more knowledge about what was coming. We watched it develop from a tropical wave to a tropical storm, gaining strength from the warm tropical waters. We soon had a powerful hurricane coming our way and in the Bahamas you can't get in your car and drive away. The harbor at Marsh Harbour is famous for its holding and we decided to ride it out there at anchor. We knew, from listening to the reports, what direction the wind would come from. We picked a position in an area of the harbor based on that wind direction and set out two anchors.

The first mate decided to check the dinghy in case we sank. The motor absolutely refused to turn over and she was adamant. We MUST have the dinghy in operating condition. Abaco Outboards suggested that we bring the big boat in to Conch Inn and they would pick up the outboard motor and fix it right away. The hurricane was still a day away, so we lifted the anchors and headed for the marina. I pulled into the large slip the marina assigned me and when I looked around--*we had a new plan*. There was a 90-foot Burger on one side of us and a big Hatteras on the other side. The docks were solid, the pilings were substantial, the wind was right on our nose and the path of the storm suggested that the wind would continue to come from that direction. We had found the right place to weather the storm.

The slip was large enough to give us plenty of room on either side. We secured the boat with two complete sets of spring lines. One set was fairly tight to hold us still in heavy wind but the second set had much more slack. If a surge occurred, we could drop the shorter lines and ride up with the long ones. The combination of two lines won't work unless you're there to make the change. In a surge higher than the longer spring lines would allow, incoming water could go completely over the boat. This is extreme, but momentary and perhaps not as bad as being lifted by an incoming surge and coming down on a piling, holing and sinking the boat.

We put chafing gear on any line that might rub. Although we were well away from the docks, we dug out every fender on the boat and set them in strategic places. All flags, canvas and cushions were stowed below and the antennas were put down and tied in place. We put tape on the windows, taped the window edges and all but one door. These storms can bring massive rainfall of ten inches or more and just rain can sink a boat. We also taped the hatches and sealed the opening for the anchor line. The inflatable was lifted out and lashed securely in place. Inside the boat, we took the same precautions we would take offshore in rough weather. Plants went in the shower and anything that might hit the deck was put away. We were ready.

The next morning, the wind whistled and then grew louder, moaning through sailboat rigging. Halyards were slapping hard against aluminum masts. The wind increased to a steady howl and stayed at that level. Heavy gusts hit the boat like a hammer and shook the doors and windows in the pilothouse. Then, almost as if Erin had lost patience, the wind piped straight up to a wild high howl like a steady chord held down on an organ. Now the winds were clocking over a hundred miles an hour. A heavy mist blew up from the surface of the water and the boats at anchor disappeared, engulfed in a fog of spray.

Boats, both sail and power, rode rough at anchor, weaving back and forth in the wind, no matter how many anchors they had out. Dinghies were burying their bows in the waves, turning over, breaking loose and losing engines. It became clear that we couldn't possibly have gotten into a dinghy in that weather. One inflatable with a strong safety line on the engine was upside down with the motor hanging down underwater. A number of boats dragged anchor, sailing down through the horrified fleet. In the marina, sails were torn to pieces when they came unfurled and Bimini tops were ripped off.

Dramatic stories unfolded all around us but we survived Erin with no great problems. We came through it OK because we knew what was coming, when it was coming and we were prepared. We knew enough to assess the situation and take advantage of every break that came our way--*and we were lucky.*

THE STORM SEASON

We try to get organized for the storm season well before the first of June. There are many predictions but storms don't have to follow rules. Most of the time, we gladly buy food and pack bags that we never use. We would rather waste our time in unnecessary preparation than be unprepared and, perhaps, devastated by a powerful storm. It's become virtually an obsession that we totally prepared for the worst and hope for the best.

We start with our storm lists, what to do and when to do it. By now, we almost know the list by heart but the list makes sure we don't forget anything. The first thing we do is get some cash and stow it in the safe. Then we dig out the maps and charts for moving the boat or the car. We decided long ago where we would head if a storm threatened. Do you know where you would go? It might be a good time to visit Aunt Harriet or head up that little river across the bay.

Next, we check to see that the water tanks on the boat are full and then head for the fuel pumps to get topped off. Starting in June, we keep the car full of gas and put together a car package for a trip that might be long and slow. We keep bottles of water in the car, as well as food that doesn't have to be cooked or prepared in any way.

This is also a good time to check out the engine room. Make sure the oil and water levels are OK in the engines, check the transmission fuel, battery levels. Now you can take your time and do a thorough job, which isn't easy if a storm is bearing down on you.

After Forty Years --- Dave Wheeler

STORM CHECKLIST

This checklist is written for our own needs but it is a guideline that can be modified to fit your boat, your family and your requirements.

AT THE BEGINNING OF THE SEASON

check hurricane lists
get cash
put jewelry, valuables and cash in safe
make travel plans for car and boat
fill water tanks on boat
fill fuel tanks on boat
check out other locations, places, slips
keep car full of gas
car package for slow travel, water, food etc.
pack toilet article kits
get travel bags out
check dry cell battery supply
lantern & flashlights
check camera film or disks
check medicines, vitamins & toilet articles
pet food & medications
food & drinks

THINGS TO PACK BEFORE LEAVING

2 flashlights & extra batteries
check all items that require batteries
two meter radio & charger
pistol & ammo
latest computer backups
wind up alarm clock
books
lantern

LAST MINUTE

get cash & package from safe
portable radio & 9v batteries
cellular & charger
laptop & accessories
telephone directory
critical files, insurance papers
all checkbooks
documentation
water, drinks
coolers
mementos or important things not to lose
wallet
glasses
car keys
pets & food
food
water
can opener, spoon, dish
medicines & vitamins
papers & records
pet bed
milk bones & toys
scissors
clippers

BOAT PREPARATION

lines & fenders, multiple anchors or solid
    mooring
chafe gear on lines
antennas down & tied
dinghy deflated, stored or tied
window protection

tape lazarette hatches
all internal items on floor, fasten in place
bike in car, in boat or stored
remove all flags
check davit is secured
tie chairs on boat deck
deck chairs inside
grill moved to secure place
clear freezer in case shore power is lost
take plants to shore

SECURE OR PUT OUT OF SIGHT

cover TV & VCR
cordless phones
VHF radios
computer, cover & unplug
cover radar, GPS and other navigation equipment
telephone recorder

Being prepared is the only answer for all the fears that come with storm season.

The local television stations will do their best to scare you to death. It's their duty. After all, they can't very well tell you to forget about it and the more appalling they make it sound, the more listeners they will have.

After Forty Years --- Dave Wheeler

Chapter Twenty-Three
FINAL THOUGHTS

All that maintenance may be a lot of work but it does keep you afloat and there's a great satisfaction in knowing that you keep your ship in Bristol fashion. Ignoring problems that aren't forcing you to do something right away, will let them grow into something far more expensive and perhaps disastrous.

Above all, if you plan to spend much time on your boat, cruise in remote areas, or even live aboard, confidence in your vessel is critical. Living aboard will make you an integral part of the vessel's system. You will learn to listen to your boat and you will know exactly what to look for when you hear a particular noise.

The assumption that people living aboard are little more than bums, is an image from the sixties that is still in some people's minds. We see sharp young people in Florida leaving their boats in the mornings, dressed in conservative suits, white shirts and tasteful ties. They're off to work as lawyers, stockbrokers or corporate executives. We see retired types reading the Wall Street Journal in the morning, sitting on yachts with every amenity known to man. Retired doctors, senior military officers or airline pilots are common and there are also some with minimum incomes who simply love being on the water. They may have small boats but the great majority are sincere, marine citizens, who take care of their boats and their environment.

Landlocked citizens are concerned about people who are so unconstrained by the dictates of society that they would sell their home and have no permanent address. The system is opposed to people mucking around on boats. It wants us conforming, cooperating and contributing. Some people think we just lay around in hammocks with tall drinks in hand, while we float down the river. That's not exactly how it is. We admit there isn't any grass to cut, but there's a lot of paint and varnish to keep up. Maybe you can let the old house go for a while, but you can't do that with a boat or it will sink. It isn't really a lifestyle for lazy people and many of these "homes" are too expensive to let them deteriorate.

In fact, many people sold houses in order to have the boat they wanted to live on. That's a serious move and it takes courage to do it. Even if you managed to buy your dream ship, there is more to do. Traveling to exotic ports of call may sound romantic and exciting, but in those strange places, there aren't any service people you know and no doctors or dentists that you've learned to trust. There will be moments of panic when something breaks or an engine dies. There will be things to fix like cranky marine toilets or things in corners almost unreachable. I work on and, sometimes, actually fix things I never looked at before. Day to day living on a boat can be inexpensive, but once in a while, there are things to rebuild or replace that will cost more than you can pay for with your regular income. Larger expenses

After Forty Years --- Dave Wheeler

may have to come out of savings or money market.

You'll meet a lot of interesting people on the water. Regardless of its size, living on a handsome boat has more class than living in a condo and you don't have to put up with association rules or people you don't like. You can move. No matter what their circumstances may be, yachtsmen are independent people who had the ability to set things up so they could live this kind of life. They like being self-sufficient and they make it work. That attitude gives them a spirit and youthfulness, regardless of their years. The mystique and traditions of the sea are bewitching and the language thrills the ears. "Two points abaft the starboard beam" rolls off the tongue with a joyous and salty flavor. Above all, you are the person in charge. This vessel is your world, your responsibility and you make it work. There are no committees out here. If there's a problem, it's your problem. If you didn't do the maintenance or made a mistake in navigation, it's your own fault.

We have been boating for over forty years and have lived aboard our trawler "Morning Star", for well over twenty years. We have no plans to move ashore. Nothing is perfect and every lifestyle has its own problems. Once in a while, when I run out of room for things or the head clogs up and dies, moving ashore doesn't sound too bad, but those ideas fade quickly when a dolphin swims in our wake. We clap our hands to get his attention and there's momentary eye contact as he rolls over and looks at us. I can't imagine where else we would want to be.

Mariners think of their boats as a living entity. They have traditionally given them female personalities. I don't know if that's a good thing, but it's indicative of the relationship that develops between a good captain and a well found boat. There is much to love in the beautiful materials, gleaming brass, stainless steel and

After Forty Years --- Dave Wheeler

golden teak. The power of well-oiled diesel engines, humming with tireless dedication, provides confidence out of sight of land. I know the solid feel of a heavy trawler crushing the waves before it into the foam and bubbles I leave in my wake. Some say we're escaping and there's a little truth to that. Sometimes, leaving a harbor, I can almost feel a weight dropping off my shoulders as I head out for the open water.

All of these things may be good excuses to go down to the sea in a ship but they are only the obvious reasons. They're the kind of things that everyone thinks of but there are things far more compelling to us. One is the weather. It's the sheer experience of being here, not enclosed in a man made shell of walls, buildings and smog, engulfed by work. On land, we were too busy to look up and see the clouds, the sky and the sun -- and we lost them, as their reflections glanced off the mirrored windows of skyscrapers and disappeared forever. Weather is the living, moving atmosphere. The rain and sun nurture us and we respond instinctively to the sound of rain pattering on the deck, waves lapping against the hull and the flutter of the flags. These are sounds of life on the water.

All of us react deeply in our guts to lowering clouds and the ominous, dark gray skies of an oncoming squall. One experiences the wet smell of the air, the sudden gust of wind and a touch of fear, as a storm marches toward you, evil and threatening. Lightning makes you wince. A few big drops splat on the deck and then the downpour smashes the water flat. The wind follows quickly like a lost temper, lashing needles of rain in your face, blurring your vision and making you bow your head in submission. You worry about what's still to come, whether you'll be far off course and just how bad the storm will get, when suddenly it stops-- just stops. The sun pops out and everything is clean and bright and it's good to be alive, to be there and see how beautiful it is.

Sometimes a storm finds us in a snug harbor with rain thrashing outside, the lines squeaking in protest and wind humming in the rigging and shredding the flags. The satisfying feeling of security, almost smugness, as the frustrated squall vents its fury outside, makes us cherish the moment.

It's being there, blessed by the best of it and threatened by the worst. Good weather is even better when you survived the bad. There is joy in knowing that your vessel is capable of dealing with bad weather and that it will take you safely to the next port. Being out on open water, out of sight of land, is a wonderful experience if you have confidence in your boat and its equipment. Seeing that first smudge of land in the distance and making landfall is exhilarating.

You can make those crossings, visit remote ports and enjoy long cruises when you know your boat will not fail you. Happiness is being on top of your maintenance and that keeps you on top of the water, no matter where you are.

After Forty Years --- Dave Wheeler

Books Published by Bristol Fashion Publications
www.wescottcovepublishing.com

Boat Repair Made Easy — Haul Out
Written By John P. Kaufman

Boat Repair Made Easy — Finishes
Written By John P. Kaufman

Boat Repair Made Easy — Systems
Written By John P. Kaufman

Boat Repair Made Easy — Engines
Written By John P. Kaufman

Standard Ship's Log
Designed By John P. Kaufman

Large Ship's Log
Designed By John P. Kaufman

Custom Ship's Log
Designed By John P. Kaufman

Designing Power & Sail
Written By Arthur Edmunds

Fiberglass Boat Survey
Written By Arthur Edmunds

Building A Fiberglass Boat
Written By Arthur Edmunds

Buying A Great Boat
Written By Arthur Edmunds

**Outfitting & Organizing Your Boat
For A Day, A Week or A Lifetime**
Written By Michael L. Frankel

After Forty Years --- Dave Wheeler

Boater's Book of Nautical Terms
Written By David S. Yetman

Modern Boatworks
Written By David S. Yetman

Practical Seamanship
Written By David S. Yetman

Captain Jack's Basic Navigation
Written By Jack I. Davis

Captain Jack's Celestial Navigation
Written By Jack I. Davis

Captain Jack's Complete Navigation
Written By Jack I. Davis

Southwinds Gourmet
Written By Susan Garrett Mason

The Cruising Sailor
Written By Tom Dove

Daddy & I Go Boating
Written By Ken Kreisler

My Grandpa Is A Tugboat Captain
Written By Ken Kreisler

Billy The Oysterman
Written By Ken Kreisler

Creating Comfort Afloat
Written By Janet Groene

Living Aboard
Written By Janet Groene

Simple Boat Projects
Written By Donald Boone

After Forty Years --- Dave Wheeler

Racing The Ice To Cape Horn
Written By Frank Guernsey & Cy Zoerner

Boater's Checklist
Written By Clay Kelley

**Florida Through The Islands
What Boaters Need To Know**
Written By Captain Clay & Marybeth Kelley

Marine Weather Forecasting
Written By J. Frank Brumbaugh

Basic Boat Maintenance
Written By J. Frank Brumbaugh

Complete Guide To Gasoline Marine Engines
Written By John Fleming

Complete Guide To Outboard Engines
Written By John Fleming

Complete Guide To Diesel Marine Engines
Written By John Fleming

Trouble Shooting Gasoline Marine Engines
Written By John Fleming

Trailer Boats
Written By Alex Zidock

Skipper's Handbook
Written By Robert S. Grossman

Wake Up & Water Ski
Written By Kimberly P. Robinson

White Squall - The Last Voyage Of Albatross
Written By Richard E. Langford

**Cruising South
What to Expect Along The ICW**
Written By Joan Healy

After Forty Years --- Dave Wheeler

Electronics Aboard
Written By Stephen Fishman

A Whale At the Port Quarter
A Treasure Chest of Sea Stories
Written By Charles Gnaegy

Five Against The Sea
A True Story of Courage & Survival
Written By Ron Arias

Scuttlebutt
Seafaring History & Lore
Written By Captain John Guest USCG Ret.

Cruising The South Pacific
Written By Douglas Austin

After Forty Years
How To Avoid The Pitfalls of Boating
Written By Dave Wheeler

Catch of The Day
How To Catch It, Clean It, & Cook It
Written By Carla Johnson

After Forty Years --- Dave Wheeler

After Forty Years --- *Dave Wheeler*

About The Author

Dave Wheeler graduated from college as an Industrial Designer and worked as an automobile designer, first for General Motors and then at Ford.

His first project at GM Styling was designing their 1955 *Kitchen of Tomorrow*. He was then assigned to their body studio where the basic car body was developed to accommodate the different divisional designs. In the automobile studios he designed the 1955 Impala coupe and the Nomad station wagon.

GM provided an interesting variety of assignments from Euclid earth movers to racing Corvettes. He became the manager of Product Analysis & Planning and wrote many of the proposals for new automobiles. When he made the proposal for the wide track Pontiac he became friends with Semon (Bunky) Knudsen. Knudsen took him to Ford when he became their President.

At Ford he designed the 1970 Mustang, set up the Design Research Studio, and ran an advanced design studio where they designed the first digital instrument panel. He was in charge of all the Designer Cars in one of his departments simply because the Designers had no idea what materials were available or what modifications might be feasible.

Ford gave him a special retirement after he lost his right leg and he and his wife immediately moved aboard their 50' trawler, Morning Star. They have lived aboard for 20 years and they've cruised from Quebec to the Exumas. He has written for some 15 magazines and a few newspapers. He and his wife live on board at Islamorada in the Florida Keys.

www.ingramcontent.com/pod-product-compliance
Lightning Source LLC
Chambersburg PA
CBHW022109150426
43195CB00008B/326